Calvin's
Preaching

CALVIN'S PREACHING

by
T. H. L. Parker

T&T CLARK
EDINBURGH

T&T CLARK
59 GEORGE STREET
EDINBURGH EH2 2LQ
SCOTLAND

Copyright © T&T Clark, 1992

All rights reserved. No part of this publication may be reproduced,
stored in a retrieval system, or transmitted, in any form or by any means,
electronic, mechanical, photocopying, recording or otherwise,
without the prior permission of T&T Clark.

First Published 1992

ISBN 0 567 29211 8

British Library Cataloguing-in-Publication Data
A catalogue record for this book is available
from the British Library

Typeset by Trinity Typesetting, Edinburgh
Printed and bound in Great Britain by Billing & Sons Ltd, Worcester

Contents

Preface	vii
Abbreviations	xiii

Part One. The Theological Impulsion

Chapter 1. The Divine Message	1
Chapter 2. The Pastoral Intention	8
Chapter 3. Scripture and Sermon	17

Part Two. The Word in Action

Chapter 4. The Preacher	35
Chapter 5. The Congregation	48

Part Three. An Account of Calvin's Preaching

Chapter 6. The Early Preaching	57
Chapter 7. Preaching in Geneva	59
Chapter 8. The Transmission of the Sermons	65

Part Four. From Exegesis to Application

Chapter 9. The Expository Method	79
Chapter 10. The Message of Scripture	93
Chapter 11. The Stimuli of Exhortation	114

Part Five. Form and Style

Chapter 12. The Pattern of the Sermons	131
Chapter 13. The Familiar Style	139

A Chronological Chart	150
Appendix 1. Catalogues of the Sermons	153
Appendix 2. Dating the Sermons on 1 and 2 Timothy and Job	163
Appendix 3. The Biblical Text	172

Bibliographies
- Sermons in Manuscript — 179
- Early French Editions — 180
- Latin Translations — 187
- English Translations — 188
- German Translations — 194
- Dutch Translations — 195
- Sermons in Supplementa Calviniana — 197
- Sermons in Corpus Reformatorum — 197
- Works by Calvin — 199
- Other Works Mentioned — 199

Index — 201

Preface

In March, 1947 there appeared a book entitled *The Oracles of God: An Introduction to the Preaching of John Calvin.* The attention it attracted was caused less, no doubt, by the presentation than by the subject. For it showed a Calvin very different from the unattractive effigy that was called 'Calvin' in the English speaking world and deservedly disliked. It even painted a Calvin whose lineaments did not look quite the same as those that one saw in the good biographies, like those by Williston Walker and R. N. C. Hunt. If they mentioned his preaching at all, it was quite incidentally, perhaps in reference to his conflicts in Geneva. Few theologians had read more than the 1559 *Institutio*, and probably not the whole of that. In general the honourable exceptions from ignorance and misrepresentation were to be found among Biblical scholars, where his commentaries were taken seriously as outstanding contributions to the understanding of Scripture.

It was not surprising that an account of Calvin as preacher should bring something new to readers and that revision was needed of the current popular view (which was almost universal; there was little scholarly work done on him in English apart from his history as a Reformer).

The book ran its course, influencing some (so I have been told in letters over the years), helping others, annoying yet others, and became out of print. Some twenty years later the publishers suggested a re-issue; but I considered that not a little revision would be necessary to bring it up to date and I could not then spare the time.

Nevertheless, the possibility of a new edition has been in the air for the past few years. The question that has exercised me is whether I could revise the book without spoiling it. Crabbèd age and youth cannot live together. If, in my mid-seventies, I started tinkering with what I wrote in my mid-twenties, would the added information swamp the freshness of the original, the removal of *bêtises* compensate for the loss of enthusiasm and liveliness?

So I decided to let well alone and to write a completely new book on the same subject. The justification for this is manifold. In the first place the general study of Calvin has made immense advances in the last half century with many very fine and perceptive books and articles in the British Isles and in America. Again, the formation of the Committee responsible for printing the manuscript sermons and the five, or six, volumes so far published as *Supplementa Calviniana*, have not only focussed attention on this preaching and brought to light some new facts and insights but have also provided new material in (what did not exist before) good scholarly editions.

But above all it has been the editing of Isaiah 30-41 for *Supplementa Calviniana* that has stirred me to write this new book. For one could not perform this editorial task without becoming fairly well acquainted with Calvin's preaching — first, the transcribing of one thousand two hundred folio sized pages of often badly written sixteenth century script, and then editing the material (earlier with Professor Lewis Thorpe and later with Professor Francis Higman — to paraphrase Kipling, 'I learnt about Calvin from them').

This book differs from *The Oracles of God* in many respects. Not only is the information fuller, so that, so far as I know, it represents the present state of knowledge on the subject, but also the whole material has been re-arranged and three chapters omitted altogether — Chapter 1. *Preaching before Calvin;* Chapter 6. *Calvin's Influence on English Preaching;* and Chapter 7. *A Recall to Fundamentals*.

The re-arrangement of the material reflects a somewhat different attitude to the subject. Instead of moving from the history of Calvin's preaching to his concept of preaching, on through stylistic considerations, and so finally to the substance of what was preached, we now start with the question of what impelled Calvin to preach, go on to the relationship between the message of Scripture and the message preached (Part One), and the responsibility of preacher and congregation towards the message (Part Two); only then do we arrive at the story of Calvin's preaching and the transmission of the sermons (Part Three); after this the way is open to discuss the way in which he handled his material (Part Four); and finally we come to the pattern and style of the sermons (Part Five).

Since this new book is rather longer than *The Oracles of God*, even including the three chapters mentioned above and the specimen Christmas sermon, it follows that the subject has been dealt with more fully. It has also been possible to use longer quotations, so that readers who are not happy with sixteenth century French and do not have the English translations of whole series readily available to them may be able to get a good flavour of what the sermons are like.

Although the book is longer than its fore-runner, its scope has been narrowed from all the sermons to five series, which will be representative of the whole corpus. These are the sets on 1 and 2 Timothy, on the latter half of Job, on Deuteronomy, and to a much lesser extent on Isaiah 30-41. Three reasons suggested the choice of 1 and 2 Timothy as the centre-pieces. First, these two epistles provide instruction, exhortation, warning, and encouragement on the pastoral task. We shall therefore learn from the sermons on them what was Calvin's understanding of his office as pastor in Geneva. Secondly, they are the only extant Sunday series whose concurrent week-day sermons (on Job and Deuteronomy) are published in their entirety. When, therefore, we have established the dates of all the individual sermons (which I have set out to do in Appendix 2) we are in possession of Calvin's daily preaching activity between September 1554 and August 1555. Thirdly, this was the period of crisis in Geneva, when Calvin's reforms faced their gravest threat and at last emerged victorious. Hence, a study of the fifty-four sermons on 1 Timothy, the thirty on 2 Timothy, sermons XCI-CLIX on Job, and numbers I-LIV on Deuteronomy, will not only afford us ample evidence for his concept of preaching but also will give a view of both his New Testament and Old Testament preaching. It will moreover give that preaching an urgency as the preacher fights for the existence of the truths he is proclaiming. If in addition we cast an eye on the set on Isaiah 30-41 we shall hear how Calvin preached when the troubles were over.

Nevertheless, it would be impossible to consider these series without an explanation of Calvin's preaching in general. Even the above paragraphs will be unclear to those who have no knowledge of that preaching: Sunday sermons and concurrent week-day sermons — what does this mean? Sermons on Job and Deuteronomy and Isaiah — surely not the whole of these books? 'Preached during the period of crisis' — were they fighting addresses against his opponents, like Puritan sermons during the English Civil War? In any case, how is it that these sermons have survived? Did Calvin write them down himself and get them printed? How many sermons are there? And above all, why did he do so much preaching?

We need to know the answers to these and many more questions before we can appreciate what was happening with the sermons on 1 and 2 Timothy, Job and Deuteronomy and Isaiah.

A word or two of explanation may not come amiss on why the final chapter of *The Oracles of God* is now omitted. It is most assuredly not because I consider that the Churches in this country no longer need to be recalled to fundamentals. On the contrary, it appears to me that the Church of England (for I have no right to speak of others) is, in almost every respect that is worth while, in a far worse state now than it was in the nineteen-forties. Doctrinally, morally, and in the understanding of its task as the *Church of — England*, the failure has been disastrous. What wonder that a Church which picks and chooses what it wants out of the Bible should become confused in its theology, flabby in its morals, and with little to state but the worldly obvious — the day after worldly liberals have stated it more convincingly?

It would, therefore, not have been difficult to find more to say on this subject today than I found in 1947. The only reasons why I have not included such a chapter are, first, that it would be, strictly speaking, an intrusion into a book on Calvin's preaching, and secondly, because it is unnecessary, in that the most of the book is a recall to fundamentals. No-one should try to preach in Calvin's manner. That would be anachronistic to the point of silliness. But if anyone, bishop, priest, or deacon, can read Parts One and Two, and in particular Chapters 1 and

4 without a blush of shame and a prayer for time for amendment of life he must be either above praise or beyond hope.

The pleasant task remains of expressing gratitude. Without doubt my chief debt of gratitude is due to Professor F. M. Higman, who not only allowed himself to be bombarded with many questions but has also read Appendix 3 and part of Appendix 2 and suggested improvements. More than that, he kindly sent me photocopies of various material not available in Cambridge. It was a comfort to know that I could turn to him for advice, encouragement, and criticism. My thanks are due also to my former research student, Mr M. D. Miles, both for pointing out some errors in *The Oracles of God* and also for letting me borrow two illustrations of Calvin's style that he unearthed. I must thank Dr P. De Klerk of Grand Rapids for help when I was preparing the Bibliography. I am grateful to the Librarian of the Bibliothèque publique et universitaire de Genève for permission to print the photographs of the specimen pages of manuscript. And finally, Dr J.-Fr. Gilmont deserves a special word of thanks. He not only allowed me to see the complete bibliographical details and notes on the sermons compiled by the late Professor Rodolphe Peter (which he is editing) but also added some vital information of his own — which incidentally saved me from advancing an ingenious but erroneous theory on one of the books.

T. H. L. Parker

Cambridge.
May, 1991.

Abbreviations

- CO Calvini Opera - Corpus Reformatorum
- EP R. Hooker: Ecclesiastical Polity
- OS Calvini Opera Selecta; ed. P. Barth and W. Niesel
- PS Parker Society
- SC Supplementa Calviniana

Part One
The Theological Impulsion

Chapter 1

The Divine Message

Sunday after Sunday, day after day Calvin climbed up the steps into the pulpit. There he patiently led his congregation verse by verse through book after book of the Bible. It is our task in this section to ask what impelled him to preach and to preach as he did.

Those who know Calvin only by repute would no doubt suppose, on hearing that he preached regularly, that his sermons were Protestant manifestos springing from the need to establish an alternative Church to Rome. Such a case could be made out quite convincingly on the basis of his position in Geneva and with the help of selected quotations from the sermons themselves. But it would come to grief on a broader examination of the sermons and it would not in any case be an answer to the second question: what impelled him to preach as he did? Why this verse by verse exposition, this teaching the Bible to the congregation, this earnest desire that the people shall conform their thinking and behaviour, not to a Protestant ethos, but to the faith of the Bible? The impulsion, or compulsion, to preach was theological. Calvin preached because he believed. He preached in the way he did because he believed what he did.

It is clear that this single-minded concentration on the Holy Scriptures could come only from a particular view of the Bible. No-one would spend so much time on a book to which he did not attach an extraordinary importance.

We therefore take our beginning at Calvin's understanding of the nature of Holy Scripture. But he devotes no part of the *Institutio* to 'the nature of the Scriptures' or 'Holy Scripture as revelation'. His views on the subject have to be sought for here and there. A convenient starting-point will be Book I, chapter vii of the *Institutio*. The theme of the previous chapters had been that, although God had left clear marks of his divinity and power on what he had made (that is, the universe) so that all men are inexcusable for not knowing and worshipping God, yet believers need a 'guide and teacher' if they are to believe that God is the Creator of the heavens and the earth. This guide and teacher is Holy Scripture.

But, goes on chapter vii, believers must be able to follow this guide, to trust this teacher, with the assurance that they will be led in the right way, taught the truth. The trustworthiness of Scripture, however, is at one with its authority. The word 'authority' is to be taken in an absolute sense; Scripture demands of right complete submission, complete credence. Whenever Calvin writes of the *auctoritas, autorité*, authority of Scripture he has in mind the thought of its *auctor, auteur*, author from whom the authority stems. It is the author, that is (as we shall see), Christ the eternal Wisdom of God, who is the 'guide and teacher' possessing absolute authority. The submission and credence, however, are neither coerced nor external but a genuine movement of the heart and mind, a joyful act of faith. This movement, this act, man, rebellious and unwilling to be taught or tamed, is unable to perform. The knowledge of the author of Scripture and thus the recognition of its authority is imparted by God himself; in other words, it is the act of the Holy Spirit. Hence the title of the chapter: 'By what testimony Scripture must be confirmed, namely that of the Spirit, so that its authority may be assured . . .'

The authority of the Bible, then, rests on 'the testimony of the Spirit'. Let us follow the argument and see what this means.

No-one with ordinary human feelings and ideas, Calvin says, will be so bold as to refuse to give credence to God when he speaks. But God does not supply day by day oracles direct from heaven. It is in the Scriptures alone that the Lord has been pleased to give a permanent form to his truth (literally, 'to consecrate his truth to a perpetual memory'). Therefore, Scripture has no other claim to full authority with believers than their conviction that it has flowed from heaven. It is as if

The Divine Message

the actual tones of God's voice (*vivae ipsae Dei voces*) were heard in it.

At this point Calvin turns to refute a current Romanist objection which a footnote in OS ascribes to Cochlaeus and Eck: It is a fact of history that the Church was in existence before the New Testament, that the books of the New Testament emanated from the Church, and that the Church determined which books should form the New Testament. It therefore follows that the authority of the New Testament depends on the authority of the Church. Calvin's reply is that this is to allow Scripture only a 'borrowed' authority, resting on human judgements. St Paul had called the teaching of the Prophets and Apostles the foundation of the Church (Eph. 2.20). The message of the New Testament (which is the point at issue, not the various forms in which it was proclaimed) existed before the Church and, indeed, gave the Church its being. Even the Canon of the New Testament was an acknowledgment rather than a determination — an acknowledgment of and a submission to the truth proclaimed by God.

But, Cochlaeus asks, how can we be convinced that Scripture 'flows from God' unless we have recourse to the Church's decree saying that this is so? Calvin brushes this aside as the typical academic question of a man without experience of faith. You might as well ask how one learns to distinguish light from darkness, white from black, sweet from sour. 'Scripture spontaneously (*ultro*) manifests as plain an idea and apprehension (*sensum*) of its truth as things do of their colour — white and black — or of their taste — sweet and bitter' (vii.2). What he means in this apparent guillotining of the debate is that revelation cannot be proved or supported by the use of extraneous arguments.

The thread of the discourse is resumed in §4 with a return to the statement that trust in the teaching of Scripture is only firmly established when we are convinced that God is its author. Hence the highest proof used everywhere by Scripture itself is that it is God who is speaking. The Prophets and Apostles do not base their claim to be heard on their own intelligence or anything of that sort, nor do they take their stand on reason. They simply refer to the holy name of God, to which the whole world is forced to submit. 'Thus saith the Lord.' No further claim is needed.

This cannot, however, be given rational proof. Certainly Calvin thinks he can demonstrate the superiority of the Bible to all other books, and this he undertakes in *Inst.* I. viii. But this is not the same as proving that God is its author. Those who attempt to prove the truth of Scripture by rational arguments are working back to front. There is only one who can prove that God is the author of Scripture, and that is God himself: 'I reply that the witness of the Spirit transcends all reasoning. For even as God alone is sufficient witness to himself in his Word, so also that Word will not find belief in the hearts of men before it is sealed by the inward witness of the Spirit. It is therefore necessary that the same Spirit who spoke by the mouth of the Prophets shall penetrate into our hearts to convince us that what had been divinely commanded had been faithfully declared' (I.vii.4).

The question has been answered: How may we be assured that the Bible demands our total obedience, that we may follow this guide and entrust ourselves to this teacher? The Holy Spirit gives believers this assurance. Hence the authority of Holy Scripture cannot be demonstrated from any grounds outside Scripture. Scripture itself asserts and demonstrates its own authority; it is αὐτόπιστον, supplying its own credibility or trustworthiness. It affects us in real earnest only when it is impressed and sealed on our hearts by God's Spirit. Then, however, we are enlightened by his power and believe that Scripture comes from God, that 'it flows to us from the very mouth of God' (I.vii.5). Every believer knows the truth of this from his own experience, he says.

The work of the Holy Spirit towards and in the Church and individual believers has been seen inescapably as occurring within Scripture. God has no commerce with men apart from Scripture. This is emphasized in Chapter ix, in opposition to some groups of Anabaptists, the sixteenth century charismatics. The title tells all: 'Those fanatics who ignore Scripture and fly off to [immediate] revelation overturn every principle of godliness.' They set the Spirit over against Scripture as appropriate for those who have spiritually come of age.

But what Spirit are they talking about? asks Calvin; the Spirit of Christ? If so, they have no case, for were not the Apostles and the early believers illuminated by the Spirit? And did *they* despise and neglect the books of the New Testament which some of them wrote and others of them read? If the Spirit is the author of Scripture, it cannot be inferior to him, nor can its teaching be in some way less than or different from his mind. He remains constant and so does Scripture. It is quite true that Scripture can be a dead letter, giving no life. But this is when it is separated from Christ and his grace. Then it will merely meet the eyes as printed words, the ears as spoken words, without its message penetrating to brain and heart. If, however, the message of Scripture is imprinted in the heart by the Holy Spirit and so reveals Christ, then it is the word of life, converting the soul.

In the final book of the *Institutio* Calvin takes up the theme again when he comes to deal with 'The power of the Church in regard to dogmas of the Faith' (IV.viii). From the first paragraph he makes his position clear: the power or authority (*potestas*) of the Church is one with the power or authority of the Head of the Church. But this must mean that the Church itself is the first to accept the authority of its Head. (All this would be tautological were it not for the unhappy fact that, whether in the sixteenth or the twentieth century, the Church too often behaves as if it thought it knew better than its Head.) Christ received of the Father that 'he should be the one and only school-master (*unicus Magister*) of the Church' (IV.viii.1). It would appear, however, that in practice the Church has had many school-masters — Moses the law-giver, the Prophets, the Apostles. But when all these were appointed to their several offices 'it was enjoined upon them that they were to bring forward nothing of their own; but they were to speak from the mouth of the Lord' (IV.viii.2). Calvin goes on to illustrate this from the Biblical accounts of the giving of the Law and the sending of the Prophets. And in § 4 he traces the line of doctrinal tradition from God the Father to his Incarnate Son, his unique and eternal Counsellor, and so to the Apostles.

The conclusion is: 'The authority of the Church is therefore not unbounded but subject to the Word of God and so to say enclosed within it' (IV.viii.4).

Calvin's next step, taking Matthew 11.27 as his theme, is to apply the truth that Christ is the one and only school-master of the Church to the stages of revelation in the Bible: 'No man has seen the Father save the Son and he to whom the Son wills to reveal him'. Therefore, whoever wishes to arrive at the knowledge of God 'must always be directed by that eternal Wisdom' (that is, the second person of the Trinity); for how could anyone either comprehend or declare the mysteries of God unless he were taught by the only one to whom those secrets are open? 'When I say this, I mean that God never reveals himself to men in any other way other than by his Son, that is, his unique Wisdom, Light, and Truth' (IV.viii.5).

Whether Patriarchs or Prophets, this was the source of their knowledge of God. But God's Wisdom revealed himself in many different ways, and at first the transmission of what had been revealed was by oral tradition. Later it was God's will that the record should be given the more permanent form of a scribal transmission. Thus the Law was written down, with strict injunctions that nothing was to be added to or subtracted from what the Lord had taught. The Prophets were not innovators, but expositors of the Law (although it is true that they added prophecies of the future). God commanded also that the spoken prophecies should be written down and so given permanence.

Hence, from the first writing down until the coming of Christ, 'the whole corpus composed of Law, Prophets, Psalms, and Histories [Psalms and Histories are reckoned as adjuncts to the Prophets] was the Word of God to the people of old; it was the rule by which the Priests and Doctors were to measure their teaching' (IV.viii.6).

But the Wisdom of God was finally revealed in the flesh; he declared openly everything that the human mind is capable of comprehending, and that is to be thought, about the heavenly Father. In place of the twilight of the time before the Sun of righteousness arose we now have perfect brightness, the full noon of the divine truth. For this is the final hour, these are the final times, the final days, from the appearance of Christ with the preaching of his Gospel until the day of judgment. The

Church has been given the perfection of Christ's teaching. With this we should be content and learn not to invent anything new for ourselves or take over anything invented by others. It is all summed up in the words spoken from heaven by God at the Transfiguration: 'This is my beloved Son; hear him' (Matt. 17.5).

We come to the final statement: 'Let this, then, be the firm principle, that nothing else is to be regarded as the Word of God and given a place in the Church than what is contained first in the Law and the Prophets and then in the Apostles' writings; and that there is no other mode of teaching aright in the Church except by the prescript and norm of God's Word' (IV.viii.8). Calvin closes this part of the chapter with a demonstration from the Apostles themselves that this was their own view of their office.

One further point is made. It might be thought that, because the perfection has come with Christ and his Gospel, the Church need not concern itself with the previous imperfection of the Old Testament, should preach only on the New Testament, even if with necessary references back to the Old for the sake of clarifying allusions and so forth. But this overlooks the main point, that the Teacher of the Old Testament Church is the same Christ as the Teacher of the New Testament Church, that the Patriarchs, Law-givers, and Prophets were illumined and inspired by the same Holy Spirit as were the Apostles. Calvin even says that the Apostles were given no further scope than the Prophets had had, 'to expound the old Scripture and show that everything taught there is fulfilled in Christ' (IV.viii.8).

Chapter 2

The Pastoral Impulsion

By turning now to the pastoral considerations that move the Church to preach we are not entering upon new ground but only presenting in a new light what has already been said in Chapter 1. The two forces, the theological impulsion and the pastoral impulsion, are so entwined that it is impossible to separate them without destroying both. They may in fact be said to be one and the same thing.

Hence this chapter will say nothing different in substance from the previous one, but, as we hear Calvin explaining in everyday language in the pulpit what he had said in the *Institutio* in a more studied manner, we shall find that the theological impulsion becomes the pastoral, yet without changing its substance at all. To put it simply, Calvin tells his congregation why he is in the pulpit and what this entails for them.

The sermon in question is Number XXIV on 2 Timothy, preached in the afternoon of July 21, 1555; its text is 2 Timothy 3.16-17: 'All Scripture is divinely inspired and is profitable for teaching, for reproof, for correction, for the training which is in righteousness; that the man of God may be whole, furnished to every good work.'

(Because the points are made so clearly we may let Calvin speak for himself at greater length either by direct quotation or by paraphrase.)

He opens by saying: 'Because the Word of God is called our spiritual sword we ought to be armed with it. For in this world the devil never stops fighting against us, to seduce us and lure us into his falsehoods. Now, to exhort us the better to do this,

St Paul here says, first, that God's Word deserves such reverence that each person shall range himself beneath it and listen to it peaceably and without contradicting. Next, he adds the profit we receive from it — and this also should move us to receive it with all reverence and obedience. Now, he is speaking principally of Holy Scripture' (CO 54.283$^{3\text{-}14}$).

There have been in all ages and there are today crackedbrains (he means some Anabaptists particularly) who do not deny that God's Word should be received without any gainsaying but yet who blaspheme against Holy Scripture by saying that it does not provide an immediate relationship with God.

But where is God's Word to be found except in the Law, the Prophets, and the Gospel? 'For that is where God has declared to us his will' (CO 54.283$^{26\text{-}27}$). 'To sum it up, St Paul here pronounces that men must not take out parts and bits that they approve of and what meets their fancy in Holy Scripture. Without exception they should conclude that, since God has spoken in his Law and in his Prophets, they must keep to the whole' (CO 54.283$^{39\text{-}45}$).

And this first of all refers to the Old Testament and not to the New. For when St Paul speaks of Holy Scripture in this place he does not mean his own writings or those of the other Apostles and Evangelists. 'At that time the only Scripture was the Old Testament. Hence we see that he meant that in the Christian Church the Law should always be preached, and the Prophets; for this is a teaching which ought to abide for ever' (CO 54.283$^{49\text{-}53}$).

This high view of preaching did not meet with universal approval either outside Geneva or within. Some, he now says, have wanted the Law cast out of the Church and be no more named. 'There were some disgusting scoundrels who a little while back disgorged their "Consummatum est" [it is fulfilled] — and that in all the taverns (I had to resist them very vehemently in my preaching); so that these rascals made up a common slogan in their — "synagogues" — their taverns: "No more Law or Prophets for us!"' (CO 54.284$^{2\text{-}11}$).

On the contrary, St Paul's meaning in this verse is that 'if we want to show our faith and obedience to God, the Law and the Prophets should rule over us and we should make them our rule and know that it [that is, the teaching of the Law and the Prophets] is a permanent and immortal truth, not decaying, not variable. God did not deliver a temporary teaching to serve a particular age; he intended it to have its force today, and would rather the world perished and heaven and earth lay in ruins than that the authority of either the Law or the Prophets should be abolished' (CO 54.284[13-25]). The last sentence is no doubt an allusion to Matthew 5.18.

So Calvin arrives at the exegesis and exposition of his text. It says two things: (1) Holy Scripture is divinely inspired; (2) It is profitable. Each is a praising of Scripture, to make it *amiable* (sweet or lovely) to us and worthy of our humble acceptance.

First, then, Holy Scripture is inspired by God. This is a declaration of the authority of Scripture, so that none shall start being rebellious against God. 'Creatures undertake war against God if they will not accept Holy Scripture. Why? "It is not of man's fabricating"; says St Paul, "there is nothing earthly here"... So much for its authority' (CO 54.284[45-53]).

Secondly, Holy Scripture is profitable. For when it pleased God to teach us by its means this was for our good and salvation.

But Holy Scripture will not be profitable 'if we are not convinced that God is its author' (CO 54.285[19-20]). If we relativise Moses or one of the Prophets, reading them purely as history and as proceeding from a mortal man, we shall certainly not feel 'the *vivacité* of God's Spirit' inflaming us. It will be dead and powerless towards us until we know that it is God who is speaking, declaring to us his will. This must be our starting point.

Papal claims of divine authority for their teaching are curtly dismissed. It is nothing but the poison of false doctrine put into a golden cup. 'But so long as any of us lets himself be governed by God he will have a good and true seal to his faith; for he will know that the things contained in Holy Scripture are not illusions of Satan, not fables invented by men, but that God has spoken and is its author' (CO 54.285[38-44]).

But there is something further: 'there is no firm authority save that of God — I mean, in the Church' (CO 54.286[1-2]). Hence we must accept only that which has the authority of God. We show that we are God's people and that he is truly our

The Pastoral Impulsion

King when we accept no other laws and ordinances [i.e. in the Church] than his, and he rules over us, and we are entirely his subjects.

So St Paul 'does not say, "Moses was an excellent man"; he does not say, "Isaiah possessed wonderful eloquence"; he does not claim anything for them personally. But he says that they were organs of God's Spirit, that their tongues were so guided that they put forward nothing of their own but that it was God who spoke by their mouth — so that we must not regard them as mortal creatures, but know that the living God made use of them and (for us be assured of this) that they were faithful dispensers of the treasure committed to them' (CO 54.286[20-32]).

The Papists claim that they speak in God's name; but in reality they do nothing but put forward their own dreams and imaginings — 'and then, that's all' (CO 54.286[43]).

Calvin now moves on from the written Word to the spoken Word, to the authority and responsibility of the preaching Church. The watchwords for preachers must be submission and obedience. 'None must presume to obtrude himself and say, "I am going to speak". St Peter wants us to have the assurance that when we go up into the pulpit we may show that God is sending us and that we are carrying the message which he has committed to us; so that "he that speaks" (says he) "let him speak as the Word of God" (I Peter 4.11) — that is to say, that he shows by what he does that he is not intruding himself at his own will and that he is not mixing in anything of his dreams, but that he has and holds the pure truth of God' (CO 54.286[51]-287[4]).

And now for the second part: Holy Scripture is profitable. We are first reminded of the purpose of this, 'that Holy Scripture may be sweet and lovely to us and that we may be inflamed with a desire and zeal to profit by it, seeing it is given to us not only to show us what is the majesty of God but to edify us unto salvation' (CO 54.287[20-25]). Who does not desire his own well-being and salvation? And where can we find this except in Holy Scripture?

The consequence for preaching is crucial: 'When I expound Holy Scripture, I must always make this my rule: That those who hear me may receive profit from the teaching I put forward and be edified unto salvation. If I have not that affection, if I do not procure the edification of those who hear me, I am a sacrilege, profaning God's Word' (CO 54.287[38-44]). The like responsibility rests upon a congregation: 'And also those who read Holy Scripture or who come to the sermon to hear it, if they are looking for some silly speculations, if they are coming here as a pastime, they are guilty of profaning such a holy thing' (CO 54.287[44-49]). For 'we ought to come to God's school with burning desire, seeing that he seeks nothing but our welfare and salvation' (CO 54.287[53-55]).

We move on to the second half of verse 16. Holy Scripture is profitable — 'profitable for teaching, for reproof, for correction, for instruction in righteousness'. Teaching on its own is not sufficient, for we are cold and indifferent to God's truth. We need to be pierced. The preacher has to use vehemence, so that we may know that this is not a game.

St Paul commences with teaching. Why? This is the natural order; we must know the truth before we can be exhorted to follow it. But we are speaking of the teaching of Scripture, the general message of the Bible. 'Now we must recall to mind what has been treated previously — what that holy teaching is of which St Paul speaks. Only this morning we saw that the aim is to know Jesus Christ, so that, putting our trust entirely in him, we may be wise by God's standard. And then earlier it was treated in prayers and supplications, to set our hope on God, to look to the life eternal to which he invites us, to mortify all that proceeds from our affections, to reform ourselves to his righteousness. Here, then, is the summary of the teaching of Holy Scripture: That we know that God has wished us to put our trust completely in him, and that we may have our refuge in him; and then that we know how and by what means he declares himself our Father and Saviour — that is, in the person of our Lord Jesus Christ his Son, whom he has given over to death for us. For this is how we are reconciled to him, this is how we are cleansed from all our stains and pollutions, this is how we are accounted righteous. And from this proceeds the trust we have to call upon God, knowing that he does not reject us when we come to him in the name of him whom he has made our Advocate' (CO 54.288[43]-289[12]).

This is the message of Scripture. It should be all that is necessary. But we are lazy and cold; we need to be 'pricked with needles'.

Hence the next word, *reproof*. Calvin apologises for using an uncommon French word, *redargution*, 'rebuke' (or perhaps in this context he intends it to mean 'conviction'): 'this word is not much used in French and I have also put *reprehension* [reproof] to be better understood' (CO 54. 289[25-27]). But the idea is right; we need to be reproved and convicted. In any case, *redargution* is a noun whose verb *redarguer* comes in I Corinthians 14.24 — if an unbeliever enters the Church and hears the teaching of God he will be *redarguez* [convicted] and judged. In other words, when an unbeliever is still in darkness and ignorance, without the knowledge of God, he is completely senseless and heedless. But when God enlightens him so that he becomes aware of the poverty of his life, he realises that he has been wicked and wretched; at that same time, if he is willing to listen to the truth of God, he so to say sees heaven opened; and he knows that men were not created for this world alone but to ascend above it. This is the way in which unbelievers are convicted.

More than that, the secrets of his heart are revealed (I Corinthians 14. 25). If the Word of God is buried, no-one looks at himself, our hearts are entangled and perplexed. 'So what are we to do? We must apply the Word of God to our use, so that we may be woken up instead of being far too sleepy; we must start giving better thought to ourselves; we must no longer put God and the salvation of our souls out of our minds but be attentive to it' (CO 54.290[1-7]). And in this way we shall be able to examine ourselves and to become ashamed of our wickedness.

The consequence of this for the preacher is that it is not enough for him to say, 'This is God's will'. For we have to be woken up and made to think in good earnest and to look at ourselves more closely and approach to God 'as if he had summoned us before his seat of justice' (CO 54.290[20-21]). Then everything will become clear and we shall be put to shame when we see our former poverty and rottenness. Then we will aspire to the heavenly life and shall not be turned away from it.

But even reproof is not enough by itself. It must be accompanied by *correction*: 'that is, that we may be, so to say, chastised by God's Word, to reform us, so that we may be drawn out of our vices' (CO 54.290[28-30]). If we have really been deeply sunk in vices the preacher must use force and violence if they are to be uprooted and thrown out. 'When a father sees his children going badly astray, he will not be content just to say to them, "What are you up to, my children?" That would be neither right nor good. He will say, "Unhappy creatures! Have I brought you up, have I provided for you until now, only for you to pay me back like this? . . . Go, wretch! you deserve to be in the hangman's hands . . . Must I nourish such scum in my house?"' (CO 54.290[45-56]). And will not God be angry with us who have behaved far worse to him than any earthly child to its father? Not, of course, that God loses his temper; but he uses vehemence to beat us down and make us submissive to him.

We can now see that it is inadequate for the preacher in expounding Holy Scripture to treat it as something in history, not even if he goes so far as to say, 'It was God who was speaking'. The faithful pastor must use vehemence and *vivacité*, 'to give vigour and power to the Word of God' (CO 54.291[26-27]). Certainly this must be done with sweetness and gentleness; but all the same it must be done. And the people must not say, 'Ho! that is too hard to be borne. You ought not to go on like that'. Those who cannot bear to be reproved had better look for another school-master than God. There are many who will not stand it: '"What! is this the way to teach? Ho! we want to be won by sweetness." "You do? Then go and teach God his lessons!" These are our sensitive folk who cannot bear a single reproof to be offered to them. And why? "Ho! we want to be taught in another style." "Well then, go to the devil's school! he will flatter you enough — and destroy you"' (CO 54.291[44-51]). But believers humble themselves and are willing to be treated severely so that they may profit in God's school.

Finally, Holy Scripture 'is profitable for instruction in righteousness, that the man of God may be complete and furnished to every good work'. Once again, this excludes all human 'instruction in righteousness'. All the Papists can say is, 'The Church has commanded this or that'. But if we wish to rule our lives aright we shall not take human ideas as our standard or rule but follow God's will — and that is found in Holy Scripture.

But there is a second point here; righteousness of life must accompany right thinking. 'To be good theologians we must lead a holy life. The Word of God is not to teach us to prattle, not to make us eloquent and subtle and I know not what. It is to reform our life, so that it is known that we desire to serve God, to give ourselves entirely to him and to conform ourselves to his good will' (CO 54.292$^{34\text{-}42}$).

The 'good works' in the text means what God calls good, not what we devise. The Papists have what they call 'good works' — fasting on saints' days and Fridays, observing Lent, serving he-saints and she-saints, traipsing about to altars and chapels, hearing Mass, going on pilgrimages. A labyrinth of nonsense! And they are not commanded by God in Scripture. We shall be furnished to every good work if we profit from Holy Scripture.

Before he ends, Calvin introduces the question: If the Law and the Prophets have such perfection (*integrité*), what is the use of the Gospel? It would seem that St Paul's teaching itself would be no less superfluous. 'The reply is easy. The Gospel was not given in order to add anything to the Law and the Prophets. Let us read, let us run through everything contained in the New Testament; we shall not find one syllable added to the Law and the Prophets. It is only a declaration of what had already been taught there. It is true that God has shown greater favour to us than to the Fathers who lived before the coming of our Lord Jesus Christ, so that things are much clearer to us now. But yet nothing has been added' (CO 54.294$^{24\text{-}35}$). Therefore, for St Paul to say that perfection of righteousness is to be found in the Law and the Prophets in no way takes anything from the Gospel. In the whole of the Scriptures of the Old and New Testaments there is 'good conformity' (CO 54.294^{39}).

This means that we have less excuse than the Old Testament believers had, in that in addition to the Law and the Prophets we have also the Gospel. The Apostle expounded everything so familiarly 'that God draws us to himself in such a way that we cannot say that we must do this or that other than what has been commanded from old time. It is necessary, then, that we apply all our thoughts, our affections, and our works to what is contained in Holy Scripture. And then we shall be approved by the heavenly Judge. And this we must do so much the more as we see that our good God has so drawn near to us, has so revealed his will, that there is no more excuse for us, and that we must cleave entirely to him'. (CO 54. 295^5-296^5).

Chapter 3

Scripture and Sermon

In our investigation into the theological and pastoral impulsion that made Calvin a preacher and the sort of preacher that he was, we have become acquainted with his view of Holy Scripture as the Word of God and of its profitability or use. Our next step must be to ask more carefully about the relationship between the Scriptures and the preacher's sermon. It has already become clear that Calvin considered that the preacher's primary task was to expound Holy Scripture, which is, so to say, the voice of God himself. But what is the nature of what is preached in the fourth or the twelfth or the sixteenth century, always supposing that its message is in agreement with the message of Scripture? Is this also the voice of God?

This question received two main answers among the Reformers. If we first consider the other answer, then Calvin's view will appear the more clearly and definitely.

The so-called *Decades* of Heinrich Bullinger, Zwingli's successor in Zürich, consist of five sets of ten sermons on various doctrines, so arranged as to present a coherent practical theology, if not an actual dogmatics. It was published in parts, the first two *Decades* in 1549, the next two in 1550, and the fifth in 1551. The collected edition appeared in 1552. We are therefore dealing with a view of preaching contemporary with Calvin's own preaching and by someone who became his regular correspondent and even colleague.

The *Decades* take the Holy Scriptures as their starting point. The first two sermons explain in what way Scripture is the Word of God; the third goes on to consider the exposition of the Scriptures. It will be noticed, therefore, that the movement is exactly the same that we have already followed.

Bullinger first defines in what sense he is going to use the term: 'in this treatise of ours, the Word of God doth properly signify the speech of God, and the revealing of God's will; first of all uttered in a lively-expressed voice by the mouth of Christ, the prophets and apostles; and after that again registered [i.e. recorded] in writings, which are rightly called "holy and divine scriptures"' (PS 1.37). 'The Word of God', then, means God's speech: the Scriptures reveal God's will, or, as the next sentence puts it, 'the word of God doth make declaration of God' (PS 1.37).

The second sermon promises that 'I will declare unto you, beloved, to whom, and to what end, the word of God is revealed; in what manner it is to be heard; and what the force thereof is, or the effect' (PS 1.57).

To whom? God has revealed his Word 'for the benefit, life, and salvation of all men' (PS 1.57). *To what end?* 'that it may teach them concerning God and his will, what, and what manner one God is towards men; that he would have them to be saved; and that, by faith in Christ: what Christ is, and by what means salvation cometh: what becometh the true worshippers of God, what they ought to fly, and what to ensue [= pursue, or follow]' (PS 1.60). *In what manner is it to be heard?* 'with great reverence', 'very attentively', 'soberly to our profit' (PS 1.64). But above all, 'We must pray continually, that the bountiful and liberal Lord will vouchsafe to bestow upon us his Spirit, that by it the seed of God's Word may be quickened in our hearts' (PS 1.66). We have been led by the third question straight to the fourth: *What is the force, or effect, of the Word?* For to speak of the Spirit is to speak of the power of the Word. 'If therefore that the word of God do sound in our ears [we must remember that Bullinger is still, at least ostensibly, speaking of Holy Scripture], and therewithal the Spirit of God do show forth his power in our hearts, and that we in faith do truly receive the word of God, then hath the word of God a mighty force and wonderful effect in us' (PS 1.67). And he proceeds to enumerate the effects in conversion, illumination, instruction, and so on. The sermon ends with the exhortation to 'beseech our Lord God to pour into our minds his holy Spirit, by whose virtue the seed of God's word may be quickened in our hearts' (PS 1.66-67).

The third sermon, which is our chief concern, starts by pointing to two contrary views current at the time. The former, that of the more obscurantist minded Romanists, 'do suppose that the scriptures, that is, the very word of God, is of itself so dark, that it cannot be read with any profit at all' (PS 1.70). In direct contrast to this the latter (no doubt but he is referring to some Anabaptists) 'affirm, that the word plainly delivered by God to mankind doth stand in need of no exposition' (PS 1.70). Consequently the way is open for the whims of private interpretation and the rejection of preaching in the Church — or, at least, of expository preaching.

To show that Scripture is not 'dark' Bullinger explains how it should be interpreted. This passage is a very brief treatment of what he handled at length and magisterially in his *Studiorum Ratio* (that is, 'The Method of Studying'). But if, as he concludes triumphantly, 'the scriptures are evident, plain, and most assuredly certain' (PS 1.72), why do they need exposition? This is not just to score a clever point off Bullinger, for this problem is a part of his whole view of preaching. All he can do at this point is to assert a fact, that is, his view that exposition of Scripture is necessary; for, following on the sentence just quoted, he says, 'But though the scripture be manifest and the word of God be evident, yet, notwithstanding, it refuseth not a godly or holy exposition' (PS 1.72). Why? 'an holy exposition doth give a setting out to the word of God, and bringeth forth much fruit in the godly hearer' (PS 1.72). But the first clause is so vague as to be useless as an explanation and the second is merely a repetition of what had been earlier ascribed to Scripture itself. To prove that Scripture should be expounded he assembles examples out of the Old and New Testaments — the prophets expounding the Law, Jesus expounding Isaiah 61.1 in the synagogue at Nazareth, Peter expounding Psalm 16.8 on the Day of Pentecost, and so on. And although he comes nearer the mark when he speaks of the need for preachers 'to apply them to the places, times, states, and persons' (PS 1.74), he has still not dealt with, far less explained, that vital link between Scripture and exposition. The rest of the sermon consists in unexceptionable instructions on how Scripture should be interpreted and expounded.

It is to be noted that Bullinger does not commit himself to any detraction of preaching in favour of the Bible. It is simply that he leaves a theological loose end between the two. The detraction was to come in a marked form many years later from Richard Hooker in Book V of the *Ecclesiastical Polity*. We may sympathise with Hooker, who was not only in his own sermons still courageously carrying the banner of the central Reformation truths at a time when many Puritans were lapsing into moralising (and trivial moralising at that), but who was also confronted by a tendency to exalt the expounding above what was expounded. Yet, even taking into account the historical context, Hooker went altogether too far in his belittling of preaching as against Scripture; or rather he, like Bullinger, failed to pay due attention to the relationship between the message of Scripture and that message faithfully expounded.

The relevant passage is Book V, xxi-xxii. He sets the context immediately: 'now it hath grown to be a question, whether the word of God [i.e. Holy Scripture] be any *ordinary* mean to save the souls of men, in that it is either privately studied or publicly read and so made known, or else only as the same is *preached*, that is to say, *explained by lively voice*, and *applied* to the people's use *as the speaker in his wisdom* thinketh meet' (EP V.xxi.1). So far, who cannot agree with Hooker? To make an either/or between Scripture and preaching, as (according to him) the Puritans did, is plainly inadmissable. Unfortunately, he swung to the opposite extreme and created another either/or.

This appears at once in his definition of the term 'the word of God', which he restricts to God's self-revelation in Scripture: 'the word of God is his heavenly truth touching matters of eternal life revealed and uttered unto men; unto Prophets and Apostles by immediate divine inspiration, from them to us by their books and writings' (EP V.xxi.2). In the main point, again so far, so good. The next step, however, is a real stride in giant's seven-league boots: 'We therefore have no word of God but the Scripture' (EP V.xxi.2). And he goes on to make an essential distinction between the preaching of the post-New Testament Church and that of the New Testament Church itself: 'Apostolic sermons were unto such as heard them his word, even as properly as to us their writings are. Howbeit not so our own sermons, the expositions which our discourse of wit doth gather and minister out of the word of God' (EP V.xxi.2).

Nevertheless, Hooker does not maintain this extreme stance. He soon takes up a both/and position and meets his opponents half-way (though it should be noted that this half-way is to be thought of in terms of Bullinger, and that in fact both the opponents and also Hooker are Bullinger-ians in this matter): 'It is on both sides confessed that the word of God [Holy Scripture] outwardly administered (his Spirit inwardly concurring therewith) converteth, edifieth, and saveth souls' (EP V.xxi.5). He narrows the issue down to a denial by the Puritans that ordinarily God works through Holy Scripture and 'our' affirmation that he works through both Scripture and preaching.

Accordingly there follows a eulogy of preaching in a piece of Hooker's choicest prose: 'So worthy a part of divine service we should greatly wrong, if we did not esteem Preaching as the blessed ordinance of God, sermons as keys to the kingdom of heaven, as wings to the soul, as spurs to the good affections of man, unto the sound and healthy as food, as physic unto diseased minds. Wherefore how highly soever it may please them with words of truth to extol sermons, they shall not herein offend us' (EP V.xxii.1).

In this same paragraph, however, the cat is let out of the bag: 'That which offendeth us is first the great disgrace which they offer unto our custom of bare reading the word of God' (EP V.xxii.1). This is not primarily a theological enquiry into the being and scope of the word of God but an attempt to justify the alleged lack of preaching in the Elizabethan Church of England. The rest of chapter xxii sets out to show how much good 'the bare reading' may and does effect. 'Wherefore when we read or recite the Scripture, we then deliver to the people *properly* the word of God. As for our sermons, be they never so sound and perfect, his word they are not as the sermons of the prophets were; no, they are but ambiguously termed his word, because his word is commonly the subject whereof they treat, and must be the rule whereby they are framed' (EP V.xxii.10).

We need pursue the matter no further. Enough has been said to make the Bullinger-Hooker view plain. The relationship between Holy Scripture and the Church's preaching has not been investigated theologically, far less determined. Sermons are left as mere explanations of Holy Scripture, as pointers to truths which exist elsewhere, as bare signs, which are necessarily separate from what is signified. It is not just coincidence that those who held a 'Zwinglian' view of the Sacraments held also the view of preaching which we have been expounding, for preaching and Sacraments are the two parts of the one action; a 'low' view of either must result in a 'low' view of the other.

Against this background of indeterminate ideas we set Calvin's clear-cut and well thought through view of the relationship between Scripture and the preaching of the Church. It is a view that in essentials he shared with Luther; and Luther scholars will be able to supply relevant quotations from their Reformer to match those that we adduce from Calvin.

There are several lines of argument that we could follow. They would all lead us to the same end and would, indeed, be found frequently to cross and intertwine. Perhaps the best and most direct is to start out from Calvin's insistence that the preacher is to invent nothing of his own but declare only what has been revealed and recorded in Holy Scripture. This is such a usual theme with him, repeated hundreds of times, that there is no need to support it with quotations. We shall, in any case, return to the subject in another section of the book. Here we fasten on the statement that the preacher shall declare only what has been revealed and recorded in Holy Scripture. By this we are referring, not to peripheral information like the age of Arphaxad or the name of the damsel who answered the door to Peter, not even necessarily to the 'great texts of the Bible' which all Christians hide in their hearts, but to the general teaching of Scripture, its essential message, which is to be found *polumerōs kai polutropōs*, 'in sundry parts and in divers manners', in all the different books (which, indeed, are only in the Bible because this essential message was recognised in them). The individual passages which together form the whole declare, in one way or another, the essential message, the self-revelation of God.

Now, granted that the preacher both understands that message as expressed in the passage that he has taken for his text and granted also that he is able to repeat the message in his own and his congregation's language and idiom, is it not plain that all he is doing is to deliver the message? The all-important factor is not whether the preacher has received the message directly from its giver or received it at second hand, but whether the message which reaches the recipient shall be the message originally given. In other words, God revealed the truth about himself and thus about men and his world to certain prophets in the Old Testament, to apostles in the New. This was the primary giving of the message; the prophets and the apostles were thus in the position of being immediate recipients, a possibility that ceased with the 'sealing up' of the New Testament. In future there could be only the secondary recipients, those who received from the first recipients. But what if the message was understood and faithfully handed on? Does it cease to be the message because it is at second hand? At the risk of labouring the point — if a man gives a verbal message to his child to deliver to someone, then, granted the child gets the message right, whose message is delivered, the child's or his father's?

For the general word 'message' which we have been using throughout, substitute 'Word of God', or 'Gospel', or (as in the Pastoral Epistles) 'sound doctrine'. It is hard to see how any of these terms has to change its character or lose part of its strength by the fact of repetition, so long as the repetition is faithful to the original.

This is not to elevate preaching to an equality with Scripture. Scripture is definitive and sovereign; preaching must be derivative and subordinate. Obviously Scripture does not have to conform to preaching; preaching must conform to Scripture. It is the humble position of preaching as derivative and subordinate that is precisely its glory.

According to Calvin, then, preaching so to say 'borrows' its status of 'Word of God' from Scripture. It is the Word of God inasmuch as it delivers the Biblical message, which is God's message or Word. But 'God's Word' means, for Calvin, that which is spoken by God; not simply in its first giving but in its every repetition. It does not somehow become weakened by repetition so as to become less and less God's Word. The Law is not attenuated in its exposition by the Prophets or later by the Apostles. In Sermon XI on Micah (the text is 3.7: 'Then shall the seers be ashamed, and the diviners confounded: yea, they shall all cover their lips; for there is no answer of God' — or, in Calvin's translation, 'they shall be confused, seeing that there will be no reply from God') he makes the same point: 'to prove all the teaching that we have now, we must come to this test. And what is it? We must consider whether what is said to us conforms with what God has left for us in writing. For what ought sermons and all teaching to be but exposition of what is contained there? It is certain that if we add anything to it, however little, it is only a corruption. Our Lord has delivered to us a perfect teaching in the Law, in the Prophets, and in the Gospel. And what, then, is it that is preached to us now? It is not that anything new is brought, but it is a more ample declaration to confirm us the more in God's teaching. *Voilà*, I say, what is the aim of all the sermons that are made to us and of all reading, so that each one may be better instructed in the will of God. And when something is put before us, we have always to ask ourselves whether it is God who has spoken or not' (SC V.89[41]-90[4]). In this last clause Calvin is not telling the people that they must remind themselves that God has spoken in Scripture but that, while listening to a sermon, they must ask themselves whether they are listening to God or a man. If the teaching is faithful to Scripture, then it is God who is speaking, and that precisely because his teaching remains his teaching irrespective of the purveyor of the teaching.

This is put more forcefully and certainly more colourfully in Sermon XXII on I Timothy (3.2: 'apt to teach'): 'For St Paul does not mean that one should just make a parade here or that a man should show off so that everyone applauds him and says, "Oh! well-spoken! Oh! what a breadth of learning! Oh! what a subtle mind!" All that is beside the point... When a man has climbed up into the pulpit, is it so that he may be seen from afar, and that he may be pre-eminent? Not at all. It is that God may speak to us by the mouth of a man. And he does us that favour of presenting himself here and wishes a mortal man to be his messenger' (CO 53.266[15-30]).

Two images that Calvin frequently used will bring out these points even more clearly.

The first is 'the school of God', *schola Dei, l'escole de Dieu.* The concept, even if not the actual phrase, informs the sections of *Inst.*IV.viii which we expounded in Chapter 1. Jesus Christ was appointed 'the unique Master' of the Church by the Father (IV.viii.1); the words 'Hear him,' applied to Jesus by the Father at the Transfiguration are a confirmation of his unique Mastership and a command to the Church in every age to teach only what he, the Wisdom of God, taught in the Old and New Testaments, whether through Law, Prophets, and Apostles or as the Incarnate Word (IV.viii.4-8).

In the sermons the usual expression is *l'escole de Dieu* rather than *l'escole de Christ*; not with any intention of minimising Christ but rather to emphasize the divine authority of the school and its teaching. And again, the term refers less to the place where the teaching is given (i.e. the pages of the Bible) than to the teaching which is given there. One further introductory remark may be useful. The word 'school', in its medieval and sixteenth century sense, will refer to university as well as to what we call a school. Accordingly, the master, *magister*, was someone with the qualification to teach; in the faculties other than the Arts it was the *doctor* who possessed that qualification. But Calvin also used 'master' for a teacher in the earliest stage, a kindergarten. These are the categories in which he was thinking of the New Testament '*rabbi*' or '*didaskalos*'.

The Greek word from which 'school' is derived occurs only once in the New Testament (Acts 19.9) and then not in a sense which would help us at present. But what is taught in the school, the *didache* or the *didaskalia*, and the teacher himself, the *didaskalos*, these are all fairly frequent New Testament words and, usefully for our purpose, they occur in the Epistles to Timothy. It will be convenient to look at what Calvin says about a few of them. These are: I Tim. 3.2, 'A bishop then must be . . . apt to teach (*didaktikon*)' — CO 53.263f.; I Tim. 4.6-7, 'nourished in the words of faith and of the good teaching (*didaskalia*) which you have followed' — CO 53.369ff.; I Tim. 4.13, 'until I come, attend to reading, to exhortation, to teaching' (*didaskalia*) — CO 53.410ff.; I Tim. 5.17, 'those who labour in the word and in teaching' (*didaskalia*) — CO 53.511f.

God is 'the sovereign Master' in his school (CO 53.263[14]). The implication is that he alone has the right to determine what is taught. He reserves this office to himself (CO 53.412[19]). Elsewhere Calvin will use the same language of Christ: 'Why do we come to the sermon? . . . It is that God may govern us and that we may have our Lord Jesus Christ as sovereign Teacher (*Docteur souverain*)' (on Deut. 1.17.CO 25.647[17-21]). But in the contexts with which we are dealing, the school is not preaching but Holy Scripture. The preacher or teacher must, before he can instruct others, first have been 'a disciple' (CO 53.263[10], 410[52]) in the strict sense of the word, one who learns from a teacher. He must first have been 'in the school of the sovereign Master' (CO 53.263[10]); he must have 'read' Holy Scripture (CO 53.410[52]) so as to have a good understanding of it (CO 53.413[22]); he must draw all his doctrine out of the well of the Law, the Prophets, and the Apostles (CO 53.410[52]). When he has done all this, he is in a position to preach to others. But he must bring to them only what he has learned (CO 53.411[14]); it must be 'pure teaching' (CO 53.263[10]), it must have been drawn out of 'the pure Word' (CO 53.512[36]). So, on the contrary side, it must not be 'secular knowledge' (*sçavoir prophane*) (CO 53.263[6]), it must not be ideas fabricated in his head (CO 53.263[7]), not his own *songes et resveries* ('dreams and reveries') (CO 53.412[19]).

If the preacher faithfully hands on what he himself has learned in the school of God, then God himself 'presides' (CO 53.264[8]), he is 'in the midst' (CO 53.264[8]), as if he were showing himself visibly (CO 53.264[18]) or face to face (CO 53.264[18]), and his people are 'joined' to him (CO 53.264[18]). Our Lord Jesus Christ is present (CO 53.264[8]) and the Church is 'united' with him (CO 53.264[8]). The pulpit is 'the throne of God, from where he wills to govern our souls' (CO 53.520[40]) (cf. Sermon 192 on Deuteronomy — 33.5: 'Let us bear in mind, then, that the doctrine which we receive of God is as the speech of a king' (CO 27.121[32-34])).

The school is God teaching in Holy Scripture; the preacher delivers to his congregation what he has been taught. So much is straightforward. But in the last paragraph above, the language becomes the language of revelation and, by implication, of redemption: God presides; the pulpit is his throne, he is in the midst, as if visible, face to face; the Church is joined to him. In other words, granted the distinction of primary and secondary which must be maintained between Scripture and preaching, the same message is powerful and effective in the one as in the other. Before that paragraph Calvin and Bullinger and Hooker were agreed; but from that point their paths diverge.

The second image is that of ambassador, taken, of course, from 2 Cor. 5.20: 'Now then we are ambassadors for Christ, as though God did beseech you by us'. Preaching on Deut. 3.12-22, Calvin feels obliged to explain how Moses could dare say that he himself had given territories to the tribes of Israel — 'Was the land his to give?' (CO 26.65[49]). But, he says, we must not find this sort of expression strange, for God's servants are not ascribing anything to themselves when they talk like this. They are showing their commission, the charge given to them, and it is on this basis that they make no separation between themselves and God. 'When a man is the envoy of his prince and has complete authority to do what is committed to his charge, he will so to say borrow the prince's name. He will say, "We are doing this; we instruct; we have commanded; we want that done". Now, when he speaks like this, he is not intending to take anything from his master. So it is with God's servants. They know that God has ordained them as instruments and that he employs them in his service in such a way that they do nothing by their own power; it is the Master who leads them. This is why Moses says that he has given this share — not claiming anything as a mortal man but as one whom God had put in his place and who did all in the name of God. *Voilà ce que nous avons à retenir.* And it is teaching which is very useful to us, for it has a still wider scope ... Why is it that we are baptized, except to obtain the washing of all our stains and that we may be pure and clean before God, and that we may be members of Jesus Christ, re-clothed in his righteousness — in short, that we may be renewed by the Holy Spirit? Now, does it lie in the mortal man who baptizes us to give us all these things? Not at all, if we consider him as a man, in his own person. But since God has willed that the ministers of his Word should baptize in his name, Baptism must have this power, even though it be administered by the hand of a man. And then, as to the Supper, we see that our Lord Jesus Christ declares that he is there, to be the food of our souls. Now, is there any creature who can make us participants of such a blessing? Certainly there is not. Now, in the same way, the Supper is not an empty disappointment. So then, when we come to receive it, we must know that the man is not separated from Jesus Christ. And in the preaching of the Word of God we see the same. It is said that the ministers are sent to enlighten the blind, to deliver the captives, to forgive sins, to convert hearts. What! these are things which belong to God alone ... For there is nothing more properly his own than to pardon sins; he also reserves to himself the converting of the heart. Now, nevertheless it is the case that he imparts all these qualifications to those whom he appoints to convey his Word and declares to them that he does not separate himself from them, but rather shows that he uses them as his hands and his instruments' (CO 26.66^8-67^7).

He goes on to make the application of the text; for what is true of God's servants in the Bible is true of his servants in post-Biblical days, even in the days of contemporary Geneva: 'So let us know that it is to our great profit that we are shown that, when God's ministers speak, they are not just uttering a fleeting sound but that its accomplishment is added to it — yes, and that our salvation is built up to that extent; when we know that the remission of our sins is not in vain preached to us daily, it ought to assure us. Do we come to the sermon? Is the grace of God presented to us? Are we shown how Jesus Christ has made satisfaction for us, to withdraw us from the curse in which we were? When all that is certified to us it is as good as if the thing itself were present with us. The reason? When God sends his messengers to announce his will to us he at the same time gives such power that the effect is joined with the Word' (CO 26.67$^{36\text{-}52}$).

Thus the minister who faithfully hands on what he has received from those who were taught directly by God is God's ambassador. No doubt an ambassador because he has been called by God and commissioned by God for this work, but also (and this is the point here) because his message is the message given by God, it is the will and mind of the Sender. The preacher is an ambassador by virtue of his message. To this extent the substance of the image is a repetition of that of 'the school of God'.

But our quotation has led us somewhat further — indeed, to the definitive point. It has become quite clear that with 'the school of God' we are not to think of preaching as a purely educative exercise, and with 'ambassadors for Christ' we are not to consider only a repetition of instructions. As in the former case, the final sentences here use the language of revelation and of the activity of the Spirit. What is daily preached in Geneva, Calvin is saying, is that God is gracious, that Jesus Christ has made the satisfaction for our sin. But when this message is preached, its reality is present and (how could it therefore be otherwise?) effective. It was not simply declared that God is a gracious God; in his Word God was being gracious in St Pierre and La Madeleine and St Gervais in May 1555. It was not only declared that Christ died for our sins, but before the eyes of the Genevans as of the Galatians fifteen hundred years earlier Jesus Christ was evidently set forth, crucified among them (Gal. 3.1). This is the language of revelation.

The reality was present, however, not through vivid imagination or the power of language, but by the working of the Holy Spirit. This is the significance of the final sentence: God 'gives such power that the effect is joined with the Word'. Some care is needed at this point, or we might slip into the error of thinking that God's Word needs power to be added to it because in itself it is powerless. In fact, it is the hearer who needs the power in order to become an effectual hearer. The message of Scripture, and hence the message of the Church in so far as it is a faithful handing on of what has been once delivered, is God's declaration of his will and thus possesses the power of God's activity, which is the power of God himself. The Word of God is never to be separated from the Spirit.

It is true that Calvin quite often speaks of the possibility of the preacher's words being mere sounds and dying on the air without having any effect. But the reason for this will be that the words are expressing only the preacher's own ideas and not the mind of God; or else he will use such an expression to assure us that in fact God's Word never is, in itself, devoid of the power of the Spirit. The comments on Heb. 4.12 bring this out clearly. Calvin's rendering of the verse runs: 'For the Word of God is living and efficacious and more penetrating than any two-edged sword . . .' He begins with the *quaestio*, 'it is to be seen whether the Apostle is speaking generally of the Word or referring it peculiarly to the elect' CO 55.49[37-39]), which he first answers by saying that the Word is not efficacious to the reprobate, whereas 'towards the elect he exerts his power so that, humbled by true self-knowledge, they flee to the grace of Christ — which cannot happen except he penetrates to the depth of the heart' (CO 55.49[41-44]). On the other hand, it may be taken as a general statement, since the Word is efficacious to the judgment and condemnation of the reprobate. And it is also in this general sense that the Word will never be preached in vain, for Christ says (John 16.8) that when the Spirit is come he will convict the world; 'But the Spirit executes this judgment by the preaching of the Gospel' (CO 55.50[29-30]). The *quaestio* is concluded with a positive statement of the power of the Word. Although it does not always exert this power towards men, 'yet it has it, in a certain sense, enclosed within itself' (CO 55.50[32-33]). But the Apostle's only intention is to tell us that our guilty consciences are summoned before God's judgment seat when God's Word sounds in our ears. 'It is as if he were saying, "If anyone thinks that when the Word of God is preached the air is being beaten with an empty sound, he is quite wrong. It is a living reality and full of a hidden energy which leaves no part of a man untouched' (CO 55.50[36-40]).

Our immediate interest in this passage is not in the two-fold action of the Word of God in condemning and saving, but only with the efficacy and validity of the Word of God. But it is clear that Calvin is using the term 'the Word' to refer primarily to any preaching, granted, of course, that it is in accord with Holy Scripture. Thus the proclamation of God's Word by way of exposition and contemporary application is itself God's Word

Scripture and Sermon

in a twofold sense: first, because the same message that was revealed to the Biblical writers is delivered by the preaching Church, and that message is God's message or Word; secondly, because the same Spirit of God who gave the message continues to ensure that that message shall accomplish in any generation what he had originally intended in giving it.

When, however, Calvin spoke of the power being, in a certain sense, 'enclosed' in the Word preached he meant no more than that, although the Word of God does not always exert its power towards its hearers, it still possesses that power. In his comments on 2 Cor. 3.6 he emphasised the other side of the matter: 'By calling himself a minister of the Spirit Paul does not mean that the grace and power of the Holy Spirit are tied to his preaching; that, so often as he wished, he could bring forth the Spirit out of his throat along with his own voice. He only means that Christ blesses his minister and so fulfils what was foretold of the Gospel. For Christ to join his power to a man's teaching is quite another matter from a man's teaching having such validity of itself. Therefore, we are ministers of the Spirit, not because we hold him enclosed and as it were captive, not because we confer his grace on all and sundry at our own will, but because through us Christ enlightens minds, renews hearts — in a word, regenerates men wholly' (CO 50.40[34-47]).

It would be misleading to attempt to construct an ontological concept of 'the Word of God and the Holy Spirit' out of the scattered places where Calvin speaks of Scripture or Gospel or preaching. He does not think of these as static forms which it is possible to sketch on two planes but views them always in terms of their movement, their activity and efficacy. Scripture is not so much the collection of writings we call the 'Holy Bible' as the living activity of God, the voice of God speaking. The message of the Gospel is the living Word coming unto his own; preaching is God calling and summoning men. All that we have heard in this chapter must be regarded in this active and forceful way: God speaks; God teaches; God governs; Christ comes to his people; Christ offers himself; the Church preaches in obedience to the commission and command; the preacher delivers the message from his prince; men submit and believe, or they reject the light and remain in darkness. Whatever the terminology used, whatever the imagery, all is a scene of divine activity, and of human activity drawn into the divine. Certainly not a feverish or a disordered activity; on the contrary, it appears with a certain steadiness and orderliness; but activity nevertheless, God's activity of redeeming the world, of forming the Body of Christ, of restoring all things.

Part Two
The Word in Action

Chapter 4

The Preacher

The office and role of the Christian preacher according to Calvin will follow necessarily from what has been said in the previous part. It has been abundantly clear throughout that the element in the Church's preaching which entitles it to be called 'the Word of God' is the message of Holy Scripture. Correspondingly, the preacher is the servant of that message. As preacher he is committed completely to the Bible. We must now see what this entails more precisely.

What is a preacher? When Calvin is talking about preaching the word that meets us at every turn is 'teaching'; indeed, this is very often used as a synonym for 'preaching'. We must at this point disregard the sharp distinction between preaching and teaching, *kerygma* and *didache*, which was such a feature of C. H. Dodd's book *The Apostolic Preaching and its Developments*. It is not simply that Calvin looked at the preacher in the context of the second quarter of the sixteenth century in Europe, when every congregation consisted largely of those baptized in Roman Catholic days; so that in the light of this the preacher's task might be understood simply as re-educating those who had been badly educated. Preaching was, for him, essentially teaching, in whatever context it might take place. Thus he will describe the New Testament *episkopos* (A.V. 'bishop', N.E.B. 'leader',) as a teacher and governor in the Church: 'Now, let us note that the word "bishop", does not stand for what they have taken it in the Papacy, for a horned animal dressed up in a mitre, with a crozier and such like toys (so that there he is just like an idol); but "pastor", "minister", "bishop", "priest" — all these in Scripture are taken for one, that is to say, for those who are called in the Church of God to teach and to govern his household' (Sermon XX, 1 Tim. 3.1. CO 53.234[3-11]).

The preacher is, then, the one who declares the teaching. We have used a circumlocution to avoid calling the preacher immediately 'the teacher', a title which belongs properly to Christ: 'Christ denies that this honour [of being called "Rabbi"] belongs to any but himself alone. Whence it follows that it is an injustice to him to transfer it to men ... The distinction must always be kept that Christ alone is to be obeyed, because it is concerning him alone that the voice of the Father resounds from heaven, "Hear him!" Teachers [*doctores*] are his ministers in this respect, that he ought to be heard in them, and they are masters [*magistri*] under him so far as they are his representatives' (Comm. on Matt. 23.6. CO 45.624[49]-625[17]). The circumlocution also, however, brings out the distinctive place of the preacher as a moment in the handing on of the message: first the message itself in the Law, the Prophets, and the Gospel; next the recording of the message; and then the contemporary delivery and explanation of the message. Thus Calvin always thinks of preaching as a *traditio*, a handing over of something received; as such, it is a moment in God's reconciliation of the world unto himself.

It is under these strict provisos, therefore, that the preacher is a *doctor*, or *magister*, a teacher, to his own particular Church. This fact is decisive for the qualities demanded in his office. It means that his conditions of service are already settled and are given to him; he does not have to create the terms or method of his work. It means also that he is given freedom, the freedom of the free Word of God (a freedom which he would regard as a restriction only if he were ignorant of revelation and faith). And it means that he is given the confidence that the message he bears does not come to him only from the tradition of his national or international Church but from Jesus Christ, the unique *Doctor Ecclesiae*.

If we investigate these conditions of givenness, freedom, and confidence we shall arrive at Calvin's concept of the preacher.

First, there is the preacher's own view of Scripture. No-one will preach happily and convincingly on the Bible who does not himself believe in the Bible; that is to say, who does not accept its teaching as the genuine expression by God of his own will and purpose. The teacher must first be a scholar. In Sermon CXXII on Job (33.3: 'my words are the uprightness of my heart') Calvin, as often, addresses directly the other preachers in his congregation: 'So then, do we wish to serve God purely in our office? We must before everything else guard our tongue so that it speaks nothing but what is printed in our heart. And indeed we hear what is said by David (and quoted by St Paul, who applies it to all the ministers of God's Word), "I have believed, and therefore will I speak". It is true that this is common to all Christians and children of God, but above all it should be observed by those whom God has set up as organs of his Holy Spirit. When we speak, *voilà* God, who wishes to be heard in our persons. Since, then, he has done us such a great honour, the least we can do is to have his teaching imprinted within us and let it take root there and then that our mouth should bear witness of what we know. In brief, we need to have been taught by God before we can be masters or doctors' (CO 35.43^{42}-44^{5}).

The preacher is, then, one who believes in and trusts Holy Scripture. This trust must be whole-hearted: 'Neither sun nor moon, light though they give to the earth, so show God's majesty as do the Law, the Prophets, and the Gospel. And yet how will people speak of it? With what audacity? I ask you, do not men today give themselves licence to speak of God's name at their own fancy? And when they start arguing about Holy Scripture over a glass of wine in a tavern or at their tables, is there any question of humbling themselves and of knowing their ignorance and their infirmity and begging God to give his Holy Spirit so that his secrets may be dealt with by us as they should be? No; those arguments are mere mockery. By this we see well enough — and more than enough — that today there is very little religion in the world. We see how some make a game of Holy Scripture, drawing it into jesting proverbs. . . . Others will discourse in flights of fancy, "Why is this? and why is that?" And then when one comes to the high mysteries of God, if they annoy us, we would like all that abolished. . . . So then let us understand that God recommends to us the honour and the authority of his Word. As if he said that we must receive in all humility everything contained in Holy Scripture, making ourselves teachable to what is contained in it. Yes, and although that might be contrary to our sense and we could wish that God had spoken in another way, we must always do him this honour of taking all our senses captive and saying, 'Lord, we are thy disciples; we receive peaceably what it has pleased thee to teach us, knowing that it is for our profit and salvation". Without exception, then, let everything contained in Holy Scripture be received with reverence; and when it is a question of the holy mysteries of God, let us not judge them according to our understanding; and if things do not seem to us to be good and proper, let us keep a tight rein on ourselves, and let God always have his way (*la vogue*) and his Word complete freedom' (Sermon XXXIII; on the third Commandment, Deut. 5.11. CO 26.281^{50}-282^{40}).

The preacher, then, is to receive 'without exception everything contained in Holy Scripture', even what his reason tells him to reject. Reason, that necessary guide in things earthly, is out of its depths in the realm of revelation and must submit to the infinite superiority of God's wisdom.

Since preaching is to be exposition of Holy Scripture, it must follow that the preacher should know the Bible well. We are not saying that he must be one of the great Bible scholars; after all, in Geneva that title could be given to only one of the preachers (or two, when Beza was present), and the others were in no way great scholars. We shall see later that the standard of preachers was, in the early days, quite low — four ministers, of whom the best educated had a poor delivery and was unable to think straight. The immediate need could be met only by importing suitable preachers. For the future Calvin looked to a solid training in the local school, from which by the fifteen-fifties were emerging suitable candidates for the ministry. They had been taught Hebrew and Greek and had been taken through enough books of the Bible to learn how they should understand the rest. They had also received a good general education as the universities then understood it — grammar, rhetoric, classical authors, mathematics, some science, history, especially Church and classical history, and what we call philosophy. The modern school-university-theological college course cannot compare in excellence with the training for preachers in Geneva (especially after the Academy had been founded in 1559), or for that matter in any good Renaissance university.

The Biblical training, however, had one very clear and well-defined aim in view: to understand the Bible as the Word believed. The tools and the methods were never given autonomy but always used to achieve this aim. There was none of the pernicious concentration on literary problems which has so bedevilled theological training in our own century — so that a bewildered student might well have conceived that the Pentateuch and the Synoptic Gospels had been composed solely to provide entertainment for minds left idle by a too-quick solution of The Times crossword. The knowledge of the Bible, so necessary in a preacher, is not a purely intellectual knowledge; it is, as Calvin was never tired of saying, 'a knowledge of the heart'. The preacher studies the Bible because he loves the Bible, and he loves the Bible because he studies the Bible. Who would want to preach on what did not move him, on what was not the lantern for his own path?

The qualifications of a preacher, according to Calvin, arise out of this single-minded, single-hearted adherence to Scripture. The first is humility, and that in two senses. Faith, or trust, in Scripture implies submission. As we have seen, it involves subjecting the reason even to anything that seems irrational. And what is submitted to inwardly is also treated as sovereign in the pulpit. To preach one's own idea is the mark of pride; not simply in that it implies that one is more clever or better informed or more spiritual than the congregation, but far more in relation to God, as showing that we know better than the Bible and thus than God. For Calvin the message of Scripture is sovereign, sovereign over the congregation and sovereign over the preacher. His humility is shown by his submitting to this authority. A sign of Calvin's awareness of this in his own preaching appears in his almost exclusive use of the first person plural and not the second, so that he does not address the congregation from some remote spiritual eminence but is ranked with them under the pre-eminence of the message of Scripture. This trait will no doubt have been noticed in the quotations we have given.

The second qualification is the outward practice of the inward submission. The preacher must himself be obedient to the teaching which he is urging on the congregation. As Calvin put it in a very lively way; 'It would be better for him to break his neck going up into the pulpit if he does not take pains to be the first to follow God' (CO 26.304[8-10]). He was very aware that he was preaching to himself as well as to others: 'When I go up into the pulpit it is not only to teach others. I do not withdraw apart; for I must be a scholar and the word proceeding out of my mouth should be of service to me as well as to you; or woe to me!' (Sermon XCV on Job; 26.4. CO 34.424[28-33]).

Thirdly, the preacher needs courage — not courage to believe but courage to proclaim the truth, however unpalatable, and to rebuke where rebukes are necessary. It is inevitable that he will arouse opposition: 'They that intend to serve God faithfully and to proclaim his Word will never lack enemies to make war against them ... Insomuch that the man who serves God in bearing his Word faithfully will never have peace nor go without stings and unmolested, nor be without many enemies'. Yet they need not fear: 'Although the world be against them and every day it seems as if they are going to be swallowed up, yet God will uphold them and break the heads of all their enemies; as he said to Jeremiah, "Go thy way! thou must fight; but thou shalt win the victory. Thou must have a forehead of brass, to oppose and resist the whole world. For in the end they shall all be broken and overthrown before thee". Since, then, we have this promise, let us hold our own and be steadfast' (Sermon CXCIV; Deut. 33.11. CO 29.154[22-40]).

Authority, the fourth of the qualifications, belongs strictly to the message and not to the preacher. Any human authority he may possess (seniority, learning, managerial experience, etc.) is very different from the authority which Calvin has in mind. It is no more than human authority, possibly matched (and therefore counterpoised and at last invalidated) by human authority of one sort or another in any member of the congregation. Moreover, such authority must always be necessarily coercive, even in the most courteous and persuasive way. The will submits to the authority, not freely and joyfully, but either sullenly or half-dazedly. It is either browbeaten or seduced. And where the choice is not free, there can be no true repentance, no faith, no conversion.

For Calvin the authority lies outside the person of the preacher and resides solely in the message that he proclaims, assuming that this is the message of Scripture. But the message of Scripture is God's own revelation of his will. Therefore, not only is the message handed on by the preacher the Word of God, but it possesses the authority of the Word of God and thus the authority of God himself. We shall never understand Calvin as preacher or the reform which he sought to carry through in Geneva unless we take this quite stupendous claim as it stands. And it is a claim advanced in the sermons times without number. There cannot be many sermons where it is not asserted explicitly or at the least implied. A few quotations will suffice.

Sermon X on Deuteronomy (1.43): 'More particularly it is said that *the people was rebellious to the mouth of God*. But how so? It is not related that God appeared in visible form, that they had heard some voice from heaven. It was Moses who spoke; it was a man who said that the people resisted the mouth of God. Now, then, we see how God wishes his Word to be received in such humility, when he sends men to announce what he commands them, as if he were in the midst of us. So the teaching which is put forward in the name of God ought to be as authoritative (*autentique*) as if all the Angels of heaven descended to us, as if God himself were manifesting (*declairast*) his majesty before our eyes ... It is true that when men speak we must weigh their words carefully. For if one were willing to receive everything that was put forward, there would be no distinction between liars and false prophets who seduce men's souls and the true ministers of God. But when we have a sure witness that what is brought to us proceeds from God (as, if we are shown by Holy Scripture that nothing is being made up but that [the preacher] is keeping to the pure simplicity of the Law and the Gospel), whoever is stubborn is certainly not making war against a creature but manifestly resists God, who wishes to be heard speaking in this way by men and making use of them as his instruments' (CO 25.713^{40}-714^{13}).

Sermon I on 2 Timothy (1.2): 'It is certain that if we come to church we shall not hear only a mortal man speaking but we shall feel (even by his secret power) that God is speaking to our souls, that he is the teacher (*maistre*). He so touches us that the human voice enters into us and so profits us that we are refreshed and nourished by it' (CO 54.11[24-31]).

Sermon XXV on Ephesians (4.11-12): 'If our Lord gives us this blessing of his Gospel being preached to us, we have a sure and infallible mark that he is near us and procures our salvation, and that he calls us to him as if he had his mouth open and we saw him there in person' (CO 51.559[24-30]).

The divine authority of the message preached needs to be examined now more closely. The quotations have shown that Calvin conceives of it as an immediate authority; that is to say, the authoritativeness consists in the fact that God is present to declare his will; it is not simply an authoritative message from one remote. It is true that this stands under the qualification of 'as if' — '*as if* he were in the midst of us', '*as if* God were manifesting his majesty before our eyes', '*as if* he himself were speaking and we saw him in person'. But what is being tacitly denied by the qualification is not the presence or the activity of God but only any sort of visible or audible perception of that presence or activity. Just as Christ is present at the Supper spiritually, that is, by the working of the Spirit, so he is present in the preaching spiritually — by the working of the Spirit.

As present, God is sovereign Lord over his Church. It is by the preaching of his Word, which is the declaration of his will, that he governs his Church and consequently guides his people in his way. This is why Calvin calls the pulpit the throne of God: '*voilà* the pulpit, which is the throne (*le siege*) of God, from which he wills to govern our souls. The seat of justice (*le siege de justice*) is certainly honourable, but when it is a question of this spiritual rule, God wishes to lead us even to the kingdom of heaven' (1 Tim. 5.20. Sermon XLIII. CO 53.520[40-44]).

The fact that God is sovereign in preaching means also that he presides as judge. The metaphor Calvin used in our latest quotation shows the way his mind is working: 'the seat of justice'. We are in the realm of 'the power of the keys' delivered to Peter (Matt. 16.19) along with the injunction (common to 'the disciples', Matt. 18.1, 18) 'whatsoever thou shalt bind on earth shall be bound in heaven: and whatsoever thou shalt loose on earth shall be loosed in heaven'; or in its Johannine form, 'whose soever sins ye remit, they are remitted unto them; and whose soever sins ye retain, they are retained' (John 20.23). The Reformers all interpreted the power of the keys as the Church's preaching. 'When we are discussing "the keys" we must always beware of dreaming up some faculty [French translation: some power given to the Church] separate from the preaching of the Gospel' (*Inst.* III. iv. 14. OS 4.101[22-24]). A little earlier in the section he uses 'the seat of justice' image: 'When the whole Church is present before the judgment seat (*tribunal*) of God, confesses its guilt and has the mercy of God as its sole refuge, it is no common or light comfort to have present there the legate of Christ, endowed with the mandate of reconciliation, from whom it hears its absolution declared' (*Inst.* III.iv.14. OS 4.100[34]-101[4]). The 'legate of Christ' is the preacher. The 'mandate of reconciliation' is the Gospel. The absolution is declared by the preaching of the Gospel. He that believes receives forgiveness; he that refuses forgiveness has his sin still 'retained' to him. Because the Gospel preached is God's Word, this is the verdict of God himself from, so to say, his judgment seat the pulpit.

To ascribe such absolute authority to preaching is clearly extremely dangerous. The opportunities for mischievous and arrogant misuses are endless. New presbyter would be a hundred times worse than old priest unless sufficient counterweights were applied. The two major counterweights have both been discussed already. They both put the preacher firmly in his place as a mere messenger. The one is that he is to put forward nothing but what God has declared in Holy Scripture; the other that he is an envoy and not the sovereign. So we find that the absolute authority is always ascribed to the message. The bearer of the message is himself humbled by its authority. It is from no merit of his that he has been chosen to be an ambassador, and he must be the first to accept the judgment in the message. 'In this he declares that the fact that he claims to have the Gospel committed to his charge was not to brag, not to exalt his merits. No, not at all. Nor was it to get a reputation among men, as if he were worthy of it. He attributes the whole to our Lord Jesus Christ' (1 Tim. 1.12. Sermon VI. CO 53.65^{43}-66^{28}). Or: 'So then, we see how it turns out with those who presume on the honour that God does them when he raises them on high. But above all, this ought to be noted in the pastors of the Church, who have the office of proclaiming the teaching of salvation. For what do we preach, save that all human glory must be thrown down and that God must be exalted in our midst? . . . And thus the principal point of the Gospel is to show men that they possess nothing to make them exalt themselves, so that every mouth may be stopped and we learn to seek all our good in God. Now since we ought to insist on that, is it not also necessary for us [i.e. preachers] to show the example of humility and modesty? . . . Let us then hold firmly that one of the principal virtues of those who have the charge of governing the Church and bearing the Word of God, is that they guard themselves from being puffed up and having a foolish arrogance which carries them away' (1 Tim. 3.6. Sermon XXIV. CO 53.285^{41}-286^{11}). Or: 'In sum, let us learn to be attentive hearers of the teaching that is presented to us in the name of God and to hear it with such humility that when we know that it is God who is speaking to us (although he uses men as his means, even men contemptible according to the flesh) we do not fail to be submissive and to show that we are truly his sheep, since he is pleased to be our Shepherd' (Titus 1.1-4. Sermon I. CO 54.382$^{16\text{-}24}$).

Nevertheless, a proper humility before God and modesty concerning himself and his capabilities are not to hinder the preacher from the bold assertion of the authority of the message he has to deliver. Indeed, it is a dereliction of his duty if he does not claim that authority. The ambassador may be no more than an ambassador and messenger but he is also no less than an ambassador of Christ, the sovereign Lord of the Church. For the message from the Lord he demands complete submission, complete acquiescence.

From all that has been said so far about the preacher flow what we may call the practical qualifications necessary for the office. If he is a teacher, he must himself know his subject; he must be a student of the Scriptures in the manner not only of literary criticism but also and far more in the way of seeking in the Scriptures the knowledge of God in Christ. As a teacher he must know how to teach; he must be able to speak in clear tones and in clear language, in language which both does credit to his subject (and does not trivialise it) and also is easily understood by his congregation. Whether he is sublime, like Richard Hooker, or familiar and racy, like Hugh Latimer, or calm and reasoned, like John Wesley, is quite irrelevant in this connection. The teacher's immediate aim is that what he is teaching shall be understood. The preacher's immediate aim is that the message of the passage he is expounding shall be understood and accepted as truth by the congregation. To know how to teach entails also a sympathy, even in a profound sense, a love for those being taught. The bully or the sneaking flatterer or the careless take-it-or-leave-it type of preacher are all in their different ways out of their proper element in the pulpit.

No sermon can be without motive. Even to preach because it is the done thing to have a sermon at a certain point in the service is a motive. But it is possible to preach without a purpose. No doubt the lower the motive the less definite the aim, the stronger the motive the firmer and more clear-cut the aim. Between the humanistic intention of Phillips Brooks, for example, with his 'preaching is the bringing of truth through personality' (*Lectures on Preaching.* 5) and the evangelical intention of P. T. Forsyth — 'the preacher invites [men] to be redeemed . . . to be reconciled to their Father' (*Positive Preaching and the Modern mind.* 5), there is the great gulf which separates the amorphous from the clearly defined. In time the amorphous aim will dwindle until neither truth nor personality remain and the sermon will become what it all too often is today, the third-hand conveyance of fourth-rate opinions.

Having heard of Calvin's well-defined views on the relationship between preaching and Holy Scripture, we shall expect to find him expressing a no less clearly defined purpose for the preacher. It is, indeed, one of his most frequent themes in his sermons, stated sometimes from the preacher's side, sometimes from the congregation's — what does the preacher enter the pulpit to do? what do the people come to listen to the sermon for? The answers will vary according to the wording of the text being expounded. So at one place in *Deuteronomy* it will be, 'Then let us make the doctrine preached to us every day efficacious (*valoir*), knowing that it is in order that God may be the better honoured among us' (CO 26.226[6-9]; on Deut. 4.39-40). And in the next sermon, 'It is God who grants us the grace that we should be taught. And why is this? ... it is in order that our life may be reformed' (CO 26.241[39-45]; on Deut. 5.1). Or more fully, on 1 Tim. 1.12: 'We who are ordained to preach the Gospel ought to know that God honoured us when he willed that from our mouth the testimony of salvation should be given to men, that we should be witnesses of his truth, that we should present salvation to those who were formerly damned and lost' (CO 53.67[38-44]).

From these quotations we gather three or four aims in preaching — to honour God, to reform lives, to witness to truth, and to 'witness to salvation' or 'present salvation'. And we could go on multiplying examples, most of which would say the same thing in the different words dictated by the different texts.

The preacher's purpose is directed first of all towards God. He preaches in order that God may be glorified. The very act of declaring the Gospel is a praising and exalting of God in his mighty acts. Every preaching of God's Word is a Te Deum Laudamus, a uniting with the heavens and all the powers therein, with the glorious company of the Apostles, the goodly fellowship of the Prophets, the noble army of Martyrs, and the holy Church throughout all the world, in the praise and worship of God. And when the purpose is directed towards man it does not lose its character of praise of God, for it is he who saves, who reforms lives, who cares for and preserves, and therefore is to be thanked, praised, worshipped.

When we come to Calvin's most frequently expressed and most comprehensive statement of purpose, it would be a travesty to regard it as some private aim of the preacher. For in the concept of 'edification' it is God who is active and effective, the preacher merely a tool that he uses. 'Edification' is one of those words debased by ill-usage. It would appear from Littré's *Dictionnaire de la langue Française* (1873) that even by the latter part of the seventeenth century it had already taken on a pietistic colouring. Littré's second definition, given a supporting quotation from Bossuet, runs: 'Sentiments of virtue and of piety that one inspires by good examples or wise discourses'. The third definition links it with teaching: 'It is often said, ironically or not, in the sense of instruction'.

Neither of these meanings or nuances goes any distance towards explaining Calvin's intention with the word. For this we turn to the New Testament original, where *oikodomeo* ('construct' or 'build') and *oikodomē* ('constructing' or 'building') are used mainly as a metaphor for the increase of the membership of the Church or its growth in holiness, or for the individual Christian's growth in holiness. It is in this primary sense that Calvin uses the word. Thus on Job 16.3 ('When will be the end of these words of wind?'), Sermon LXII: 'He calls "words of wind" where there is no resolution (*fermeté*); that is to say, which cannot *edify* a man, as Holy Scripture uses that similitude. For when it is a question of a man being taught for his salvation it is said that one *edifies* him. How? In that he is *founded* and then afterwards that one *builds* on it, so that he is confirmed in the fear of God, he is confirmed in the Law, he is confirmed in patience to bear afflictions steadfastly, and then he sets his mind on praying and calling upon God, of having recourse to him' (CO 34.5^{47}-6^1). Or, 'And then, when a man will be a preacher, it is not just a question of making a sermon, but in general and in particular it is necessary for him to know that it is to proclaim the Word of God in order to *edify*, so that the Word may be profitable' (1 Tim. 3.1. Sermon XX. CO $53.236^{42\text{-}46}$).

Chapter 5

The Congregation

The preacher is only the half of the Church's activity of proclamation. He has received God's message from Holy Scripture and is now handing it on to others. These others, the members of the congregation, form the other half. Now, it is a strange fact that, although there are hundreds, perhaps thousands, of books written about the preacher, the hearers have been largely neglected. The assumption seems to be that, whereas the preacher is really doing something, the people have a passive role, like so many jugs waiting to be filled. Commonsense and experience should teach us that this is untrue. Anyone who has regularly preached over many years but then has been a member of a congregation for some time, would (if he had strong views on preaching) be hard put to it to decide which was the more demanding, preaching well or listening properly.

Calvin certainly expected the congregation to be active in the business of the Church's preaching. For preaching is a corporate action of the whole Church; it is a specific act of the worshipping Church. In the same way, therefore, as each Christian participates in the activity which is the Lord's Supper, taking and eating the Bread, receiving and drinking the Wine, so also in the audible Sacrament which is the sermon he actively hears and takes into himself the Word of God. It is true that the preacher gives and the congregation receives; but the reception is not passive, but an active participation, a listening that is an act of faith. The people should bring with them to church a right frame of mind, desiring to hear the voice of their Good Shepherd speaking to them what he knew they needed

The Congregation

needed to hear. As we heard in Chapter 2, 'we ought to come to God's school with burning desire'. No doubt some, knowing what verses would be treated tomorrow, studied those verses in readiness. But Calvin never (so far as I have noticed) suggested that they should do this. He does, however, frequently urge the people to come well-prepared to the sermon.

The principal thing is that the congregation shall have a clear idea of what Christian preaching is and therefore of what is happening in the sermon. In the following remarkable passage from Sermon IV on Deuteronomy (1.17. 'the judgment is of God') we see Calvin moving from Scriptural image to Scriptural image, from book to book of the Bible, from Deut. 1 to Matt. 17.5, to Ps. 78.52 (and the many Old and New Testament parallels), to John 10.3-5, to Matt. 11.7 with Eph. 4.14, to 1 and 2 Timothy, and at last by way of allusion to 1 Pet. 5.8-10: 'all Christians ought to think, "Why do we come to the sermon? Why is there [this] order in the Church? It is so that God may govern us and that we may have our Lord Jesus Christ as Sovereign Teacher, so that we may be the flock that he leads (*le troupeau de sa conduite*)". Now, that cannot be unless we all hear his voice, distinguishing it from the voice of strangers; so that we may not be carried here and there like reeds shaken by every wind, but may be stayed on the purity of Holy Scripture and our faith so grounded there that the devil will never shake it' (CO 25.647[17-29]). We are plainly very far from any thought that people should attend sermons in order to receive religious uplift or comfort or to be given 'devotional' or 'spiritual' answers to their problems. They should consider that in the sermon God rules his Church by declaring his will, that Jesus Christ himself teaches them as the good Shepherd calling his flock.

When Christians know what preaching is, they also know what their attitude to it must be. Their representative and leader, the preacher, has been the first to submit completely and unconditionally to the message of Holy Scripture. They can do no less when that message is passed on to them. As we have seen, Calvin adds the necessary caveat at this point: The congregation is not to listen uncritically, accepting anything and everything, but is to be sure that what is preached really is the message of Scripture. It may be thought that this presupposes perhaps an élite congregation, certainly an adult and thoughtful congregation. But such an objection in turn presupposes and accepts as normal the sort of situation which is common today, when a preacher with little interest in the Bible sermonizes to a necessarily untaught and therefore bewildered or apathetic congregation. In this situation preaching creates a particularly vicious circle. Calvin, however, has in mind a congregation that has been taught Christian truths from childhood; by the time they have reached years of discretion they should certainly be able to tell chalk from cheese. If they cannot, then (granted they are of sound mind) they betray that they have little interest in the Faith they profess.

Granted the caveat, the congregation is to be completely submissive to the message from God, good pupils at the feet of their 'sovereign Teacher', Jesus Christ: 'when we come to hear the teaching that is declared to us in the name of God, we must be prepared in humility and fear to receive all that is said to us and to give heed to it and not to bring a spirit of gall, a spirit full of rebellion or arrogance or pride; but let us know that we have to do with our God, who wishes to test the obedience and subjection that we owe him, so often and whenever he calls us to him' (Harmony of the Gospels; Sermon XXIV. CO 46. 286$^{28\text{-}38}$). But we are not talking about the natural receptivity that is expected of anyone who attends a lecture on any subject. With preaching it is a question of revelation, of God appearing as Judge and Saviour, and of 'righteous' man being unmasked as the sinner he really is, repenting and believing. This is the fundamental element in whatever is being taught in the pulpit. Consequently, the submission to God's message is the work of grace, not of nature. And as the work of grace, it needs to be prayed for and striven after — striven after in the sense of mortifying our rebelliousness against God's Word: 'By this word ['with meekness'] he signifies the modesty and easiness of a mind composed to learn. Isaiah describes it when he says, "On whom does my spirit rest save on the humble and quiet?" [57.15]. So few make progress in the school of God; for scarcely one in a hundred will renounce the fierceness of his spirit and submit quietly to God . . . But if we desire to be the living planting of God, let us take pains to submit our minds in humility and allow ourselves as his lambs to be ruled by our Shepherd' (Comm. on Jas. 1.21. CO 55.394[4-14]).

As the work of grace, this submission to God's Word is the work of the Holy Spirit. We have come, by a different route, to the point that has been definitive in each of our earlier chapters — the inward witness of the Spirit. It is God's Spirit who makes a man ready to be taught by his Word: 'When we come to hear the sermon or take up Holy Scripture to read it, let us not have this foolish presumption of thinking that we shall easily understand by our own wit everything that is said to us and that we read; but let us come with reverence, waiting entirely on God, well aware that we have need to be taught by his Holy Spirit, and that without that we can in no way understand what is shown us in his Word' (1 Tim. 3.9; Sermon XXV. CO 53.300[6-16]).

It is by God's Spirit that the congregation desire to hear God's Word preached to them, that they recognize it as God's Word and distinguish it from all other words, and that they believe and become 'doers' of the Word. Without this attitude of submission and expectancy, this *piété, pietas*, the fear of God, all our turning the pages of Holy Scripture, being preached to from morning to evening and then spending the night in meditating what we have heard, will be like water running off us: 'Do we want, then, as I have said, to profit in the school of our God, so that his teaching may be useful to us and we may be edified by it? Let us always have this foundation — it is that we try to devote ourselves to the obedience of our God, that he may be exalted in the midst of us, that he may have the reverence he deserves. When that happens we shall be building well' (1 Tim. 4.7; Sermon XXXI; CO 53.382[4-11]).

It follows that the congregation no less than the preacher have a responsibility towards what is taught. But this goes further than their own response to it. They, no less than the preacher, have a duty to see to it, so far as they can, that the message of the Bible shall alone be heard in their pulpit (for the pulpit is the pulpit of the whole Church, not merely of one member, the preacher). As most Churches are constituted, this will be a matter of encouragement or discouragement rather than of command, for the power of congregations is both limited and indirect. What Calvin has in mind is that the congregation shall look for and be pleased to receive God's message and not make the preacher's task harder by asking for this or that alien fancy: 'Now, just as many preachers are themselves far too given to ambition and in order to find grace and favour seek only what will please, so also on the other side the people are the cause of making preachers swerve aside from the good way. And why? Because, as St Peter says [in fact, 2 Tim. 4.3] men have "itching ears" and want to be fed with pleasing stories and buffoonery or "old wives' fables", as St Paul calls them here. Seeing that men have such desires — like pregnant women whose cravings are inordinate — ah well! this is the cause of some preachers degenerating and disguising themselves and transforming God's teaching, which is as bad as destroying it' (1 Tim. 4.6-7; Sermon XXXI. CO 53.371[49]-372[2]). And then, a little later in the same context: 'So then, do we want those who have the charge of teaching us to speak plainly and be ready to show us the way of salvation? From our side [we remember that for one week in two Calvin was not in the pulpit but in the congregation] let us not seduce them to evil and be the cause of their transforming the teaching of God. And how? let us not be given over to foolish cravings and fly up into the air, but let us seek to be edified' (CO 53.372[35-43]).

The congregation, therefore, no less than the minister, should have a clear purpose in mind when they set themselves to listen to the preaching. Certainly, the purpose can only be general, or congregation and preacher, both with excellent but dissimilar specific purposes, would be at *cross*-purposes. The specific purpose will be determined by the particular passage of Scripture; so that in this respect preacher and congregation might be termed chameleons, taking their colour from whichever passage they are perched on. The clear general purpose, shared by preacher and congregation, is edification, the building up of the believer in the knowledge and love of God and thus the building up of the Church into God's holy Temple.

Once again, however, we must note that Calvin has no idealistic first-curacy sort of belief that every member of the congregation is a fully sanctified and whole-hearted lover of God's Word, the one hundred and nineteenth psalm personified. How it actually was in Geneva we shall see in a later chapter. But his realism is shown by the frequent exhortations to become teachable, to humble themselves to receive God's teaching, to do violence to their own natural inclinations, to mortify their pride. Even the best grounded and most experienced Christian is still a sinner, preferring his own ideas and ways to God's teaching. If this week he loves the sacred Word, next week he may feel cold and uninterested; worst danger of all, he may feel bored, knowing it all already. The task of the congregation, as Calvin portrays it, is a continuous life-long battle against their own rebelliousness, apathy, and arrogance in favour of God's teaching and call. The members of the congregation, no less than the preacher, need continually to pray, 'Come, Holy Ghost!'

Part Three
An Account of Calvin's Preaching

Chapter 6

Before 1541

The intimate knowledge that we have of Calvin's preaching is only of that which took place between 1549 and his death in 1564. Before then the information is sparse and the number of surviving sermons very few.

Stories have come down of occasional preaching before 1536. In his *Vie de Calvin* (1565) Colladon tells us that 'before he departed from France it is certain that Jean Calvin, although not in priest's orders, began to preach a few sermons' at Pont l'Evêque, a village just outside Noyon of which he held a curacy (and his father's birthplace) (CO 21.121[34-42]).

From Colladon also we learn that Calvin preached at Lignières, a village near Bourges, while he was studying at Bourges at the end of the fifteen-twenties. The fact that Colladon was himself a native of Bourges adds credit to the story: 'At the same time he preached sometimes in a little town called Lignières in the country of Berry, and was welcomed at the house of the then squire, who (not understanding any different) just said in general that it seemed to him that M. Jean Calvin preached better than the monks and did a pretty lively job' (CO 21.55[41-48]). This anecdote bears the marks of being a family joke among the Colladons; perhaps it was to them that the squire spoke — 'Your young friend M. Calvin . . .'. The story is repeated and embellished by much later writers (see Doumergue: *Jean Calvin* 1.191).

Credible also is Colladon's statement that, while in retirement from dangerous Paris at Saintonge in 1534, Calvin wrote some '*formulaires de sermons et remonstrances Chrestiennes*' (CO 21.56[51]-57[1]) which his host, Louis du Tillet, gave to various local curés to use for preaching, 'in order to give the people some taste of the true and pure knowledge of salvation by Jesus Christ' (CO 21.57[1-3]). The earlier preaching at Lignières was perhaps the enthusiastic outburst of feeling from the newly converted. This work at Saintonge shows the already mature Christian teacher; indeed, it is far from fanciful to see in these 'model sermons and Christian addresses' the core of the first edition of the *Institutio*, completed the following year and published in March 1536.

Calvin's regular preaching career began when he consented to remain in Geneva in September 1536. Even then, however, he was at first unwilling to become a pastor and agreed only to lecture in theology (CO 21.58[51-52]). Yet it was not long before he changed his mind: 'but a little later he was also elected pastor' (CO 21.58[53-54]). Thus he embarked on his two-fold office of lecturing and preaching in Geneva. Of the lecturing at that time we have a little information (that he expounded St Paul's epistles), of the preaching none save that he was said to have called the City Council 'a council of the devil' (CO 21.222[32-38]).

There is a similar scarcity of information about his preaching in the French Church in Strasbourg after his banishment from Geneva in 1538. There, too, he continued his lecturing on the New Testament. In welcome contrast to his experiences in Geneva he found a congregation friendly and appreciative. It would appear that he preached four times a week — presumably twice on Sundays and once on two other days (CO 10a.288[30-31]).

Chapter 7

Preaching in Geneva

It is not until his return to Geneva in September 1541 that a definite picture of Calvin's preaching begins to emerge. The *Ordonnances* establishing the ecclesiastical side of the constitution of Geneva laid down specific instructions on the four orders of Christian ministry — pastors, doctors, elders, and deacons, corresponding to the spheres of the preaching ministry, the education of youth, the exercise of discipline and social welfare. The city was divided into three parishes, St Pierre, St Gervais, and la Madeleine, which were to be served by five pastors with three assistants. The pattern of services was that there was to be a *sermon* (that is, a service with a sermon) 'at daybreak in St Pierre and St Gervais, and at the customary hour' (that is, in the afternoon) in all three churches (*Registres* I.5). During the week there were to be sermons on Monday, Wednesday, and Friday, staggering the times so that the service in the one church should be ended before the next church began. This service also was held in the morning, but obviously the third church would be at least two hours later than the first. Daybreak was interpreted as 6 o'clock from Easter to October 1 and as 7 o'clock during the winter.

We see Calvin, then, established as the minister in charge of St Pierre, the former cathedral. But we still have little information about his preaching. No doubt the regulations of the *Ordonnances* were followed in St Pierre, but we do not know how often he himself preached. There is a glimpse of a characteristic action in the first sermon after his return: 'When I preached to the people, everyone was very alert and expectant. But, entirely omitting any mention of what they were sure they would hear, I gave a brief account of our office. To this I added a moderate and modest commendation of our faithfulness and integrity. After this preface, I took up the exposition where I had stopped, indicating by this that I had only temporarily interrupted my office of preaching and not given it up entirely' (OC 11.365[49]-366[4]). It was on Easter Day 1538 that he had stopped, and September 1541 when he went on to the next verse as if it were only the following day. From this, however, it is clear that his sermons were already expository and, it would seem, already connected series on whole books of the Bible.

The following July he was reporting the state of things to Farel. Four ministers had been elected and would prove suitable enough when they had had more practice. The one best educated, however, had a poor delivery and confused ideas. The other three were making good progress but were not, of course, a patch on Viret (whose return to Lausanne had left Geneva considerably the weaker). This meant that Calvin had to increase his own preaching: 'Those who want to make progress also wish me to preach more frequently. I have already started to do so and shall continue until the others have become more acceptable to the people' (CO 11.417[27-36]).

This seems to have laid a heavier burden on him than he could sustain, for on September 11 the Council noted that 'Sr. Calvin ought to be exempt from preaching except once on Sundays' (CO 21.302[23-30]). It is not clear whether this means only one Sunday sermon as well as the three in the week or only one sermon in all.

Only six, or perhaps seven of his sermons have survived from these years, for of the *Quatre Sermons* on 'Subjects very profitable for our times', published in 1552, three were preached before 1549 (see SC VI.p.XXIII). To understand what is about to be said, we must interpolate now a few facts about the attempted recording of Calvin's sermons before 1549. Their outstanding quality was early recognised and several hearers made notes of them for their own edification. Besides this, some more or less official secretaries, like Jean Cousin, Nicolas des Gallars, and François Bourgoin, tried to record individual sermons or whole series. Thus two of the sermons mentioned above were taken down by Jean Cousin (the first on Ps. 115

occasioned by news that 'the Papists have started a war in Germany against the Christians' the second, on Ps. 124, on hearing the news of the victory of Philip of Hesse and his allies). Des Gallars took notes of the expository sermons on Isaiah and Genesis and, combining them with notes of Calvin's lectures on those books, wrote the commentaries which were published under Calvin's name. The names of a few others who tried to record sermons have come down to us — Charles Joinvillier (who led the group recording Calvin's lectures), André Spifame, André de la Chesnaye, Jacques Dallichant, and Laurent de Normandie. Colladon shows the shortcomings of these earlier attempts: 'It is true that several had formerly exerted themselves to do this, both with the lectures and the sermons. But they had not reached the stage of taking it all down word for word and really did little more than record the principal points without following the thread of the subject' (CO 21.70$^{35-41}$). And Calvin voiced his own misgivings in a letter to M. de Falais: 'M. Maldonad has spoken to me about Jacques [Dallichant], as to whether he could take down my sermons. From what I have seen [of his work], he gets some sentences well; but the substance is less full than I could wish — although in time he could improve and do better.... Someone more apt may turn up in time' (CO 12.540$^{21-31}$).

The *Quatre sermons* are not verbatim recordings but revisions into a literary style. As Calvin says in his preface, 'I have thought it best to revise and arrange a sermon which I had preached on this subject and of which the substance had been taken down' (CO 8.373/374). He writes in the same vein when he sends a copy of the *Exposition du Pseaume 87* to King Edward VI: 'As I was expounding [this psalm] one day in a sermon, the argument appeared to me so suitable to you, that I was immediately induced to write out the whole ... It is true that I treat the subject in general terms, without a personal address to yourself, but I have only had reference to you in writing it' (*PS Original Letters* 2. 714). Taking the words at their face value, it would seem that Calvin did not revise a secretary's notes of his sermon but wrote out in a literary form what he had preached, sent one copy to the king and kept another for publication.

The title of this written-up sermon moved Rodolphe Peter

to place among the sermons a little publication of Calvin's entitled *Exposition sur l'epistre de sainct Iudas* (1542). This is not impossible, for its substance seems closer to preaching than to a contribution in a *Congrégation*. If we accept the theory, it will mean that Calvin preached a sermon, or possibly two, on Jude in 1542. As there is nothing in this *Exposition* to suggest that the sermon (if sermon there was) was called forth by some special need or event, we may accept that it was preached in the ordinary course of things. And if that is true, it would seem reasonable to suggest that after his return to Geneva in September 1541 he preached through the Canonical Epistles (which, moreover, do not occur among the books treated after 1549). But, of course, this is conjecture.

From the year 1549 everything changes for us. Before, we have to do our best to make bricks with very little straw at our disposal. Afterwards, we have a harvest load of straw, as much, perhaps, as we know what to do with. The frequency of sermons was changed in the October of that year from three during the week to one every day. Not that every minister had the heavy task of preaching twice on Sundays and once every week-day; even Calvin restricted himself to the two Sunday sermons and every day of alternate weeks, or rather, that was his general pattern of preaching. Sometimes, as on Deuteronomy, he preached from Monday to Friday of alternate weeks with an additional sermon on the intervening Wednesday. The Sunday sermons seem to have been preached in St Pierre, but those on weekdays were sometimes given in one of the other churches.

We shall appreciate the magnitude of Calvin's work as a preacher if we remember that each of these sermons was about an hour long and that his preaching was only a part of his pastoral duty. We may let Colladon, who lived in Geneva through these years, tell us of his labours: 'Calvin for his part did not spare himself at all, working far beyond what his powers and regard for his health could stand. He preached commonly every day for one week in two. Every week he lectured three times in theology. [In fact, the lecturing was also normally in alternate weeks, when he was not preaching.] He was at the *Consistoire* on the appointed day and made all the remonstrances. Every Friday at the Bible Study, which we call the *Congrégation*, what he added after the leader had made his *declaration* was almost a lecture. He never failed in visiting the sick, in private warning and counsel, and the rest of the numberless matters arising out of the ordinary exercise of his ministry. But besides these ordinary tasks, he had great care for believers in France, both in teaching them and exhorting and counselling them and consoling them by letters when they were being persecuted, and also in interceding for them, or getting another to intercede when he thought he saw an opening. Yet all that did not prevent him from going on working at his special study and composing many splendid and very useful books' (CO 21.66[19-41]).

The sermons were now recorded and even carefully catalogued. We therefore now learn that the Sunday sermons were on New Testament books, the week-day on the Old. The only exceptions were that for a period on Sunday afternoons he preached on the Psalms and (perhaps every year?) would on a festival interrupt the current series to preach on an appropriate text. Thus from Sunday to Saturday of Holy Week in 1549 he preached on Matthew chapters 26 and 27 and on Matt. 28 on Easter Day. In the two following years he took the story of the Passion and Resurrection from St John; from an unspecified Gospel in 1553 and 1554; and from St Matthew again the next year. All the Whitsun sermons we have are on Acts 2, all the Christmas sermons on Luke (no doubt Chapter 2). Apart from these, however, his sermons were continuous expositions. He began at chapter one verse one of a book and continued with one or a few or many verses for each sermon until he had got to the end of that book. Then the next day or the next Sunday he started on another book.

We can therefore follow his course through the next fifteen years. At the opening of 1549 his Sunday sermons were still on Hebrews and Psalms, his week-days' on Jeremiah. After Hebrews came Acts, lasting until March 1554. Jeremiah, meanwhile, was succeeded by Lamentations in 1550; which completed, eight of the Minor Prophets took him into 1552. Soon after Job had commenced, on February 26 of 1554, he reached the end of Acts and then of the Psalms. Thereafter the same book served for morning and afternoon; first, 1 and 2 Thessalonians, and then 1 Timothy. This gave place to 2 Timothy in April 1555, by which time he had completed Job and turned to Deuteronomy. Titus came after 2 Timothy, but 1 Corinthians next from October 20, 1555 until February 1557. Meanwhile July 15, 1556 had seen the end of Deuteronomy and July 16 the start of Isaiah (this was the second time he had preached on Isaiah). From 1 Corinthians until Ephesians Calvin followed the common New Testament order, bringing him to 1559, when in July he began to preach on a Harmony of the Gospels and in September on Genesis. The Gospels sermons occupied him on Sundays for the rest of his life. Concurrently with these ran week-day sermons on Judges in 1561, on 1 Samuel from August 1561 until May 1562, on 2 Samuel until February 1563 and finally on 1 Kings.

Colladon gave a moving account of his last few determined weeks of pastoral activity: 'Finally, his gout began to abate somewhat, and then he forced himself to go out sometimes to be entertained among his friends, but chiefly to lecture and even to preach, having himself carried to church in a chair. He also presented some children for baptism when asked. Even about mid-January he led the [study of the] beginning of the Prophet Isaiah in the *Congrégation* at the request of the other ministers... Thus he continued to do all he could of his public office, always dragging his poor body along, until the beginning of February 1564. For on Wednesday, February 2, he made his last sermon on the Book of the Kings and at 2 o'clock in the afternoon his last lecture in the school, that is, on Ezekiel. And on the Sunday, February 6, his last sermon on the Harmony of the three Gospels. Thereafter he never went up into the pulpit' (CO 21.96[4-23]).

Chapter 8

The Transmission of the Sermons

It will be remembered that over the years sporadic and unsuccessful attempts had been made to record the sermons. In 1549, however, the matter was put on a more business-like footing and a professional stenographer was sought by the committee called *La compagnie des étrangers* — 'The Immigrants' Society' we might loosely translate it. This society had been formed to help the refugees who flocked into Geneva in ever-increasing numbers, chiefly from France but also from other European countries and from England in the reign of Mary Tudor. But the French naturally felt a special relationship with Calvin as their fellow-countryman and it was chiefly from them that the impetus came to give the sermons and lectures a more permanent form.

La compagnie des étrangers did not have far to look for a suitable candidate. A refugee had come to Geneva from Bar-sur-Seine; his name Denis Raguenier. For some little while he had been taking down Calvin's sermons for his own use. Using a private system of short-hand that he had evolved and perfected, he showed that he was capable of discharging this difficult task. As a married man, moreover, with a family to maintain, he could do with the money, even though the *compagnie* could not pay very much — about half the stipend of a minister.

This is not the place for a history of short-hand writing. Sufficient to say that a system had been known and successfully employed from the first century B.C. onwards but, strangely enough, had dropped out of use by the period that might have been thought to make good use of it, that is, the twelfth century. The Middle Ages seems to have used a sort of combination of speed-writing and contractions. It was not until 1588 that what is recognisable today as a system of short-hand was published and thereafter came many, some fairly successful, some failures, until Pitman's well-known system appeared in 1837.

Raguenier's name does not appear in histories of short-hand (presumably because his achievement was not known to the authors), but it is clear that he had perfected an efficient system forty years before the first modern method, explained in Bright's book, *Characterie: an Arte of Shorte, Swifte, and Secrete Writing by Character*, which appeared in 1588. The precise nature of Raguenier's system is unknown. We learn only from one source that he employed 'certain notes and characters' (CO 25.587[33]) and from another that he wrote '*par nombre et chiffre*', 'by number and figure or cipher' (CO 49.XVIII). For his accuracy we do not need to rely on the witness of his contemporaries. The uniformity of style from sermon to sermon, coupled with the same uniformity in the sermons recorded after his death, is sufficient testimony. The modern editors of the sermons for *Supplementa Calviniana* need to make amendments only infrequently, and indeed, we usually find that such errors as occurred arose not at the short-hand stage, but at the subsequent writing out in long-hand by a scribe.

Raguenier's achievement will appear all the more remarkable if we bear in mind the conditions under which he worked. He had to record about six thousand words in an hour, often at break of day, whatever the temperature in an unheated church, whatever the light, using a quill and ink (pencils not having been invented until 1564), and to keep this up morning after morning.

His work was not finished, however, when the sermon was down in his short-hand notes. The next task was its transcription into long-hand manuscript. For this he had the assistance of a number of scribes. Either he or an assistant first wrote out in fair hand the serial number of the sermon, the date on which it was preached, the Biblical text, and the first line of the sermon. Then, we conjecture, he must have dictated the sermon from his short-hand for the scribe to write it down. It is hard, almost impossible, to believe that any of the scribes would be able or trusted to decipher his short-hand, at least for a few years. When the series on the Biblical book was completed, the manuscript was usually bound as a volume and placed in the charge of the Deacons, who granted access to it at their discretion. Some series or parts of series were printed a few years after their preaching.

We have spoken of Raguenier's accuracy and the completeness of his recordings. It was said that even from the start 'hardly a word escaped him' (CO 25.587[33-34]). But this is going too far. A careful examination of the sermons in their chronological order reveals a striking improvement in his ability to record the whole sermon. He began work officially on Sunday, September 29, 1549, but it would seem that he had been recording the series on Acts from its start on August 25, and even before that the sermons on Jer. 14-18 between June 14 and August 16. These latter have survived and are printed as *Supplementa Calviniana VI*. The average length of these sermons is about two-thirds that of those preached five years later. Moreover, the Biblical text is indicated only by the first verse. As there is no reason to suppose that Calvin preached shorter sermons at that time and did not announce the whole of his text, the reasonable assumption is that Raguenier was still not quite equal to his new task. This assumption is confirmed by an increase in the length of the two extant sermons on Lamentations. By the time Micah was reached on November 12, 1550, Raguenier was able to record the whole sermon. But even by the end of Micah he was still not giving more than the first verse of the Biblical text, followed by 'etc.'. On the other hand, it is possible that for the Jeremiah sermons, intended only for himself, he was content to record only the substance, and that he did not at first perceive the importance of recording the whole of the Biblical text.

Raguenier died either in the latter part of 1560 or early in 1561. The recording of the series on the Harmony of the Gospels was broken off at the place he had left it, the sixty-fifth sermon. Another stenographer was found and he recorded (using Raguenier's method?) the week-day sermons until

Calvin ceased to preach. Those on 2 Samuel (the only one of these series now extant in French) are of the average length for Calvin's sermons, showing that the stenographer was recording the whole sermon. The only difference from those taken down by Raguenier after 1551 is that the Biblical text is not given in full but breaks off with some such formula as 'until the end of the sixteenth verse', or, 'finishing with the words, "And the munitions of war are perished"'.

The first catalogue was made by Raguenier himself in 1557 and kept up to date until his death (See Appendix 1 part 1 for a translation). Although it contains several slips, this must be regarded as the only authoritative catalogue of the manuscripts until recent times. In 1613 the Rector of the Collège asked that the sermon manuscripts should be transferred from the care of the Deacons to the regular library (SC II.p.XIX). This was agreed to; but the library catalogue of 1620 makes no mention of them. They do, however, appear in the catalogue of 1697, where the total number of volumes is put at forty-eight, a figure we need not take seriously, as is shown in Appendix 1, part 2.

Nearly a century later, in 1779, Jean Senebier, who was now librarian, prepared a new catalogue of manuscripts in the Bibliothèque. Introducing his own errors into the calculations, he now presented us with forty-four volumes. (See Appendix 1, part 3).

Raguenier also compiled a catalogue of sermons on Church Festivals. (See Appendix 1, part 4.)

The reader who is unacquainted with what happens next will be impatiently wondering why we do not simply write to the Bibliothèque publique et universitaire de Genève and settle the matter once and for all. Alas! the catastrophe has not yet been recounted. In the year 1805, Senebier was instructed by the directors of the Bibliothèque to sell to the booksellers Cherbuliez et Manget a copy of any books of which the library possessed duplicates. When he did so, he also threw in the manuscript sermons for good measure. A correspondent to the local newspaper, le Journal de Genève (which ran a campaign of protest — but only twenty-one years later!), supposed that little importance was attached to the manuscripts because, first, they were not in Calvin's own hand, secondly, 'they were very difficult, not to say impossible, to decipher', and finally because the library kept one volume and also had a large number of manuscripts in Calvin's own hand. M. Gagnebin adds two further reasons — the urgent need for more shelf space at the time and the fact that the sermons were viewed as extemporary commentaries and thus as mere repetitions of the regular commentaries (SC II.p.XXI). One volume, however, was kept as a specimen.

Post tenebras, lux! is the motto of the City of Geneva. So it was now, even though the light was but a rush candle. The 'unparalleled fatality' of the disappearance of 'this so precious collection', as le Journal put it, at least called attention to the existence and value of the sermons. But it seems to have been by a happy chance that two theological students (probably Guillaume and Adolphe Monod — a famous name in French theology) came upon eight of the volumes in *une fripière*, which I take to be a junk shop. They bought them (by weight) and gave them back to the Bibliothèque.

So now there were nine. Soon another volume joined them from a source unknown to us.

In 1846 the library of J.-P. Maunoir was put up for auction in London. Two of our volumes were included and were bought by a bookseller, Mr Barret, for £4.15. They found their way back to the Bibliothèque twelve years later. These volumes contained, (1) some sermons on Psalms, with sermons of Viret on Isaiah, (2) sermons on the Passion of Jesus Christ, together with some *Congrégations* (not sermons, as the sale catalogue said) of Calvin and Cop on Joshua. The total at this point is twelve.

In 1887 the third volume of Isaiah was given to the Bibliothèque by M. Tronchin, who had received it from his grandfather, who had received it from a M. Theremin, who had bought it from the booksellers Cherbuliez et Manget, to whom the manuscripts had been sold in the first place.

A fourteenth volume, this time a presentation copy from Raguenier to the city council on the occasion of his being made a citizen in 1556, was returned to the Bibliothèque in 1879.

In 1957 the Committee responsible for *Supplementa*

Calviniana instituted a search for the missing manuscripts. None came to light. But the Bodleian Library disclosed that they possessed a presentation copy of the sermons on Genesis. This had been made by Raguenier for the City Council to present to Thomas Bodley himself when a student at the Academy of Geneva.

A few years later (1963) the pulse of life in my quiet country vicarage was quickened by the receipt of a letter from the Librarian of Lambeth Palace, saying that he had recently bought a manuscript volume of Calvin's sermons on Genesis from Bristol Baptist College; would I please see them and pronounce on their authenticity. This, of course, I was only too willing to do.

My friend and colleague Richard Stauffer, whose untimely death cut short his editing of the sermons on Genesis, described this as 'une découverte non moins étonnante' than the Bodleian revelation (*Les Sermons Inédits de Calvin Sur Le Livre de la Genèse*, 27). He concluded that the Lambeth volume was not one of those sold in 1805 but, like the Bodleian manuscript, a presentation copy. Its particular value lay in that it supplied the first five sermons on Genesis, omitted from the Bodleian copy; but it ended with the twenty-fifth sermon, whereas the Bodleian continued to the ninety-seventh (*Les Sermons Inédits*, 29ff.).

Two further manuscript volumes containing sermons by Calvin are known to exist. The Bibliothèque Nationale in Paris has a collection of letters with five sermons included — on a Psalm, on verses from Genesis, and on odd passages. The Burgerbibliothek of Bern has a copy of the sermons on Ephesians; this manuscript was made by André Spifame in 1560, presumably from the original manuscript, for the first printed edition is dated 1562.

The total number of sermons in manuscript, not counting duplicates or earlier printed copies, is about 680, according to M. Gagnebin (SC II.p.XXVIII). It is difficult to arrive at a precise figure. My own figures would make 680 a maximum.

Our account of the transmission of the sermons will not be complete, however, until we have spoken of the printed editions. It is very clear from the number of manuscript copies that were made that there was a considerable demand to possess copies of the sermons. But by the fifteen-sixties publication by manuscript was a thing of the past. Calvin himself was, as we have seen, at first unwilling that these extemporary productions, possibly imperfectly recorded, should be given the permanence of printing. Nor was he ready to devote considerable time to the task of revision. Perhaps what chiefly caused him to change his mind was the evident value of the sermons to the French Evangelical churches (it was, after all, chiefly they who would be able to read sermons in French) as well as the obvious competence and reliability of Raguenier's work.

Most of the sermons published in Calvin's life-time were selections from a complete series. From *Genesis* there were those on Melchisedech (1560), Abraham's sacrifice of Isaac (1561), and Jacob and Esau (1562). From *Isaiah* came Hezekiah's song after his sickness (1562), and Isaiah 52.13-53.12 (1558). From the scattered and sporadic sermons on the Psalter were those on Ps. 119 (1554). Those on the Ten Commandments (1562) were taken from *Deuteronomy*; from *1 Corinthians* were chosen the sermons on chapters 10-11 (1558). There was also the collection of occasional sermons on '*la Divinité, Humanité, et Nativité de nostre Seigneur Iesus Christ*' (1563). A few complete series appeared—*Job* (1563), *Galatians* (1563), *Ephesians* (1562), and the *Pastoral Epistles* (1563).

All these were sermons taken down by Raguenier when he had become thoroughly experienced in his task. It is worth noting that all the printed editions, whether extracts or complete series, were (with the sole exception of *Daniel*) of sermons preached between 1554 and 1562 and that (now with the exception of *Plusieurs sermons*) they were 'Raguenier' sermons.

After Calvin's death there followed *Deuteronomy* (1567) and *Daniel 5-12* (1565), which was, in fact, printed without permission at La Rochelle.

Those series mentioned so far were, apart from the *Quatre Sermons,* in French. In order, however, to reach an international readership two were translated into Latin. These were *1 Samuel* (1604) and *Job* (1593).

When we turn to the dissemination of the sermons by translation into the modern tongues we are confronted by a surprising fact. Apart from the French speaking communities, it was not the Europeans who were interested in Calvin's sermons but the English. The only European translations to be made were: one in Italian (the *Quatre sermons*, 1553); four in German (the *Quatre sermons*, 1586, *Job*, 1587-88, the concluding prayers in *Job*, 1592, and *Ps. 119*, 1615); and in the Netherlands a volume of miscellaneous sermons in 1598 and the sermons on Melchisedech, justification, and Abraham's sacrifice (1604).

In contrast to this paucity, no fewer than thirteen of the eighteen printed editions appeared also in English, as well as three sermons not printed in French. The exceptions were the *Exposition sur . . . sainct Iudas* (1542), the incomplete and pirated *Daniel* (1565), the Latin translation of *1 Samuel* (1604), and some of the occasional sermons included in *Dixhuict sermons* (1560). Thus, all the complete sets recorded and printed were translated into English, together with the several selections made from the sets.

Some volumes had more than one edition. The *Quatre sermons*, widely read on the Continent, appeared (either *in toto* or in part) in no less than five forms and in three or four different translations. *Job* was printed twice in its first year, again after five years, and yet again five years later still.

Precise details will be found in the Bibliography (pp. 188-194), but it is worth drawing attention here to a few relevant considerations. First the chronological pattern is inconsistent, with a strong concentration of editions in the fifteen seventies and eighties. Counting the new editions and impressions together, the numbers are: 1550-1559, 1; 1560-1569, 3; 1570-1579, 11; 1580-1589, 7; 1590-1599, 1. Interest in Calvin's sermons followed the general pattern of the rise, flowering, and decline of his influence in England.

Secondly, it is worth looking at the names of the translators. Among them Arthur Golding stands out in the quality and bulk of his work. He translated four major series — *Job* (1574) was his first large scale translation from French, *Galatians* (1574), *Ephesians* (1576), and *Deuteronomy* (1583). It is for his verse rendering of Ovid's *Metamorphoses* into 'fourteeners' that he is usually mentioned in histories of English literature (a work which Shakespeare knew and borrowed from). Golding writes a strong, energetic prose, keeping close enough to the original to do justice to Calvin's own style.

Slighter in quantity and quality were the translations of Thomas Stocker. He was responsible for the sermons on Ps. 119 (1580), for the *Divers sermons* (1581), and for those on Melchisedech (1592). The only major series not translated by Golding was that on the Pastoral Epistles, and this was undertaken by Laurence Tomson (1592), who also translated the New Testament from Beza's edition. For the rest we find a few well-known names and some little known. Robert Horne, the Bishop of Winchester, got his *Certaine homilies* translated and published in 1553, just after the accession of Mary had made the publishing of evangelical books hazardous. It was therefore published as being 'Imprinted at Rome before the castle of S. Angel at the signe of St. Peter'. Anthony Munday, who revised Horne's translation for an edition in 1584, was the prolific Elizabethan and Jacobean playwright and ballad writer (or more strictly, poet in ballad form). He, too, supplied Shakespeare with some good lines, apparently even the famous 'making the green one red' — but this was not from his translation of Calvin. William Warde, who saved the *Thre notable sermons* (1562) from extinction, was Professor or Reader in Medicine at Cambridge and was also a physician to Queen Elizabeth. John Harmar, translator of the set on the Ten Commandments (1579) was Professor of Greek at Oxford.

We have, therefore, translators who were, although not household names in English literature, nevertheless all of good repute and most of them experienced and competent writers. Calvin was not at all badly served by his English translators.

Behind the translators were the backers, those influential persons to whom the volumes were dedicated. To have the patronage of the Earl of Leicester ('Elizabeth's favourite', but not for much longer) for *Job* and the *Ten Commandmentes*, of William Cecil for *Galatians* and of Robert Cecil for *Melchisedech*, gave a certain air of authorisation which would dispose those who were swayed by big names to lend Calvin their ear. At any rate, it meant that the sermons entered on their English career with the privilege of powerful support.

Apart from the unrepresentative *Quatre sermons*, *1 Samuel*, and *Job*, all of which were included in Latin in the *Calvini Opera Omnia* of 1617 and 1667, the sermons were left unpublished after the last German translation of 1615 until a selection from those on the Pastoral Epistles appeared in Philadelphia in 1831 (a revision of Laurence Tomson's translation). Calvin's sermons were, in effect, unknown to the seventeenth and eighteenth centuries and to half the nineteenth.

When the enormous task of preparing a more thorough edition of all Calvin's works was begun for the series *Corpus Reformatorum* in 1860, the editors at first intended to fulfil what the title of their work promised: *Opera Quae Supersunt Omnia. Ad Fidem Editionum Principum et Authenticarum Ex Parte Etiam Codicum Manu Scriptorum... ediderunt* — 'All the extant works, edited reliably according to the first and authentic editions and also partly according to manuscripts'. When, however, they actually cast eyes on the fourteen large manuscript volumes with the usually extremely difficult handwriting, their hearts failed them and they contented themselves with the easy task of including only sermons already printed. Certainly students of Calvin should be grateful to have so many of his sermons in a more accessible form than the rare sixteenth century editions. Unfortunately, however, *Corpus Reformatorum* fails to do justice to the sermons. The headings, giving the date of each sermon, together with the full Biblical texts, are often omitted, as are also the concluding prayers. No attempt is made to identify references. Worst of all, the whole is vitiated with numerous errors. In editing the *Sermons on Isaiah's Prophecy* (1956) I collated *Corpus Reformatorum* with the first edition and found just on two hundred errors in their ninety-four columns. Although some of these were merely orthographical, enough genuine errors remained to show that, at least for this particular series, it could not be used for serious study with confidence.

Not until 1931 did the sermons receive the attention they deserved. In that year the book *Die Predigt Calvins* by Erwin Mülhaupt appeared. Although he dealt mainly with the printed sermons, Mülhaupt brought to light the extent of Calvin's preaching and directed attention to the manuscript volumes in Geneva. This book influenced another German scholar,

The Transmission of the Sermons

Hanns Rückert, who had already begun to take an interest in Calvin's manuscript sermons. He set himself what anyone who has worked on these manuscripts would consider the impossible task of transcribing, editing, and publishing the whole lot. He began with the first manuscript volume, which happened to be *2 Samuel* and his edition was published in 1936.

There, however, matters rested until after 1950, when the Presbyterian World Alliance asked Dr J. I. McCord, at that time in Austin, Texas, but soon to become President of Princeton Theological Seminary, to form a committee to see to the editing and publishing of the manuscript sermons. The committee consisted at first of J. I. McCord as chairman, E. Mülhaupt as principal editor, G. A. Barrois, J.-D. Benoît, B. Nagy, T. H. L. Parker, H. Rückert, and R. Stauffer. They were joined in due course by O. Fatio, R. Peter, L. Thorpe, and F. M. Higman.

Four volumes have so far been published (besides a new edition of the original *2 Samuel*): *Isaiah 13-29*, edited by G. A. Barrois (1961); *Micah*, edited by J.-D. Benoît (1964); *Jeremiah 14-18 and Lamentations 1*, edited by R. Peter (1971); *Psalms and Sermons on Festivals*, edited by E. Mülhaupt (1981). The sermons on *Isaiah 30-41*, edited by F. M. Higman, T. H. L. Parker, and L. Thorpe, are at the time of writing with the printers and will perhaps appear before this book. Editors are at work on the other manuscript volumes. A list of the extant sermons is given in the Bibliography.

Part Four
From Exegesis to Application

Chapter 9

The Expository Method

Expository preaching consists in the explanation and application of a passage of Scripture. Without explanation it is not expository; without application it is not preaching. There can be Christian preaching which is not expository in the sense we have given; otherwise we should have to withhold the title of Christian preaching from Peter's sermon in Solomon's porch (Acts 3.12ff.) and Paul's in Athens (Acts 17.22ff.). Moreover, of those sermons recorded in Acts which must be called expository, there are different patterns. Philip seems to have expounded the short passage Isa. 53.7-8 to the Ethiopian eunuch, whereas Stephen (Acts 7.2-53) and Paul (Acts 13.16-41) ran through the Old Testament as a whole. We may therefore say that although all Christian preaching must be an unveiling of the message of Holy Scripture, yet that unveiling can legitimately take more than one form.

The classical form, of which Origen is usually regarded as the first exponent (see for example, *Geschichte der christlichen Predigt* in *Realencyklopädie* 15.630[4ff.]), consisted of the explanation of a short or long passage of Holy Scripture. This form is still recognised as the proper way of going about things; it is still usual to read a verse or clause of Scripture as preface to the sermon, even if it has no discernible relevance to what follows in the sermon itself.

Within the classical form there are varieties, as we may easily see by looking at collections of sermons. Spurgeon usually preached on isolated texts, perhaps taking a striking phrase as his main subject; so also did Newman in the *Parochial and Plain Sermons*. The liturgical year provided another way, with the epistle and gospel for each Sunday. A large proportion of Luther's sermons are of this type, the *Kirchenpostille über die Episteln* and those *über die Evangelien*. Newman's sermons on the Christian Year on the other hand (*Parochial and Plain Sermons* vols. 5-6) were on individual verses from anywhere in the Bible applied to a particular season. Latimer sometimes, and Lancelot Andrewes more often, followed the course of the Church's Kalendar.

There is yet a third style of expository preaching, a style which was practised especially in the fourth and fifth centuries. It consisted of expounding whole books of the Bible, passage by passage. Thus Chrysostom preached through most of the books of the New Testament and his younger contemporary Augustine expounded the Psalms and the Fourth Gospel. Although in the four or five centuries preceding the Reformation the Bible was far from absent from preaching (we need think only of the Biblical homilies of Anselm, Bernard of Clairvaux, Bonaventure, or Thomas Aquinas), the broad scope of connected series largely dropped out. It was, however, continued in the class-room of the theological faculties, where verse by verse exposition of complete books was the regular method. When Calvin, therefore, embarked on this course (following the practice in Strasbourg and Zürich) he was taking up the tradition of the later Fathers and of the medieval theological training.

Almost all Calvin's recorded sermons are connected series on books of the Bible. As we have seen in the previous chapter, he preached on a New Testament book on Sunday mornings and afternoons (although for a period on the Psalms in the afternoon) and on an Old Testament book on weekday mornings. We must now examine his expository method more closely.

We see him, then, on high in the pulpit (how often he speaks of 'mounting up' into the pulpit, of being 'in an eminence' or 'on high', of being 'seen from afar'!). Before him is his Bible — but before we go further we must ask what we mean by 'Bible'. A French Bible? a Latin Bible? a Greek Bible? a Hebrew Bible? It has been one of the puzzles exercising the minds of the editors of *Supplementa Calviniana* from the beginning that

The Expository Method

in some series of sermons the French Biblical text does not agree with the text of any French version known to us and that when repeating a text he often does so in a different rendering. The Introductions to the various volumes show that the problem has not been resolved uniformly if resolved at all. It may be felt that the editors of SC III, on Isaiah 30-41, present a convincing case; this is, that when preaching on the Old Testament Calvin translated his text direct from the Hebrew. From this it may be deduced that on the New Testament he preached from the original Greek. (The whole argument is too complicated to explain now and would interrupt our present theme. It is set out in Appendix 3.)

He had, then, a Hebrew Old Testament or Greek New Testament before him and preached without any notes (or so we assume from the fact that he had no notes when he lectured). This was not from any notion that extemporary preaching was superior to a written sermon or notes, but no doubt because he knew he could trust his memory. He did, however, regard preparation as necessary: 'if I should climb up into the pulpit without having deigned to look at a book and frivolously imagine "Ah well! when I get there God will give me enough to talk about," and I do not condescend to read, or to think about what I ought to declare, and I come here without carefully pondering how I must apply the Holy Scripture to the edification of the people — well, then I should be a cock-sure charlatan and God would put me to confusion in my audaciousness' (On Deut. 6.16. Sermon XLIX. CO 26.473^{54}-474^{8}). His preparation therefore consisted of a study of the passage to be expounded — not usually too arduous a task, especially if he had already written a commentary on that book or had lectured on it — a consideration of how he should treat it, and above all, of how he should apply it to that congregation at that particular time. This is stored in his mind as he mounts up into the pulpit.

The first sermon on any book dealt wholly or in part with the general theme of that book. It was therefore a very simplified form of the *Argumentum* of a commentary, omitting the finer points of criticism unless they were directly relevant and concentrating on the chief subjects that would arise. From the outset the book is made both universal and particular, lifted from its original setting, seen as covering all men in all ages and then focussed upon 'us today'.

Let us take some examples of introductory sermons.

Deuteronomy. God gave his Law at Horeb after he had brought his people out of Egypt. But the people were disobedient and would not keep the Law. 'Now, in the end God again determined that there should be a definitive summary of the Law, and that it should be confirmed — as it is confirmed in this book. And this is why it is called "Deuteronomy", which is equivalent to "the Law repeated". Not that God has brought in anything new; but he has reproved the people for the malice that we have spoken of . . . As when some children have done badly at school and have been dreadful donkeys, when they have had a year without getting any further forward they have to go back to their ABC . . . Now then, we see in the sum what is the argument [theme] of this book . . . Now, all that we see in that people applies to us' (CO 25.607^{43}-608^{33}).

Ephesians. Here Calvin goes straight into the application. 'In reading the Epistles which St Paul wrote to this or that place, we must always think that God intended them to serve not only for one time or for certain peoples, but for ever and the whole Church in general . . . The sum of this epistle which I have now undertaken to expound is . . .' (CO 51.245$^{4\text{-}16}$).

In *Job* also Calvin's first words bring the book firmly to bear on 'us': 'In order to profit well from what is contained in the present book, we must first of all understand the sum of it. Now, the story written here shows us that we are in God's hands and that it is for him to ordain concerning our life and to dispose of it according to his good pleasure . . .' (CO 33.21$^{6\text{-}12}$). God has complete dominion over all his creatures and will bring to pass what he knows to be best. Job is an example to us and we should follow that example. The outcome of all his sufferings was happy, and so will it be with us if we accept God's good will. The sermon then goes on to explain the whole book in a nutshell. God gives the suffering but it is brought by the devil, who has his instruments to work by — Job's three friends and his wife. Through them Job's physical sufferings became spiritual temptations and sufferings — the thoughts that God was his enemy and would show no mercy. But the clue to the understanding of this book is to realise that Job has a good case but pleads it weakly and misguidedly, whereas his friends have a bad case, but plead it highly efficiently. Calvin will remind us of these themes continually throughout the book. The introduction is not quite ended, however, for the authorship of the book is touched on — according to some Jews (i.e. Rabbis) it was Moses. But this is uncertain, so we will leave it undecided. Next, where was Uz? Perhaps the Land of Edom; which would mean that God had a faithful servant among the unbelieving descendants of Esau. Then, what does the word 'Job' mean? perhaps 'weeping', perhaps 'man of enmity'. And finally, this is a true story, not fiction.

2 Timothy. This is an epistle which traditionally is placed during Paul's imprisonment at Rome. Calvin makes use of this to give an aided poignancy to the epistle. His introduction perhaps at first betrays a little awkwardness in reconciling the poignancy with the divine authorship. In the end it may be the poignancy and his own predilections which win. 'Although in all the writings which St Paul has left us we must consider that it is God who spoke to us by the mouth of a mortal man and that all his teaching ought to be received in authority and reverence, as if God showed himself visibly from heaven, yet there is in this epistle something special to be remarked; it is that, St Paul being in prison, seeing his death near, he here wanted to confirm his Faith as if he had sealed it with his blood' (CO 54.5$^{4-13}$). If we read the letter with this in mind, he goes on, we shall find that God's Spirit has expressed himself in it with such majesty and power that we cannot help being 'as it were ravished' by it. 'As for me, I know that this epistle has profited me more than any other book in Scripture — and still profits me every day' (CO 54.5$^{24-26}$). If we want to have a witness of the truth of God which will 'pierce through our hearts', we can well settle down here. A man would have to be quite asleep or utterly stupid if God does not work in him when he hears the doctrine drawn from it.

Micah, however, demands some attention to Old Testament history. In his first lecture on Micah (CO 43.281$^{24-30}$) Calvin would stress the importance of knowing the historical context;

without such knowledge Micah's discourses would at least come out somewhat weak, if not quite useless. So now in the sermon Calvin sketches the circumstances under which Micah wrote and who were his contemporaries. But even in the course of the explanation he digresses to 'Now, the prophets certainly served their own times; but, as St Peter says, their teaching is addressed to us today; and St Paul even says that they looked especially to our time' (SC V 1[29-31]). After developing this point he returns to the history.

The introduction to any book, however, seldom takes long and then Calvin can go on with the exposition. His text will vary in length from a single verse to a whole passage of perhaps ten or a dozen verses. Not infrequently he will preach two or three consecutive sermons on one verse; thus, thrice on 2 Tim. 1.8 and on 1 Tim. 2.5, while 1 Tim. 3.1-4 lasted for four sermons. But the general rule was for two to four verses a sermon; Micah, whose seven chapters constitute one hundred and five verses, occupied twenty-eight sermons, or between three and four verses a sermon; 2 Timothy and Isaiah 30-41 come out at about the same number.

It is worth remarking that, on those books on which Calvin preached and wrote a commentary, the divisions that he made in the chapters — that is, the verses taken in a sermon and those forming a division in the commentary — tally fairly closely. Take 1 Tim. 1 as an example:

Commentary	Sermons	Number	
1.1-4	1.1-2	I	a.m.
	3-4	II	p.m.
5-11	5-7	III-IV	a.m. & p.m.
	8-11	V	a.m.
12-13	12-13a	VI	a.m.
14-17	13b-15	VII	p.m.
18-20	17-19	VIII	a.m.
	18-19	IX	p.m.
	19-20	X	a.m.

Here we see that the commentary sets of vv. 1-4 and 5-11 are followed but sub-divided between Sermons I-V. Thereafter, however, the groupings differ. It would seem that, for his New Testament sermons, Calvin may have planned for Sundays as a pair rather than for individual sermons. Thus, on September 16 the set is vv. 1-4, on September 23 vv. 5-7 and so on. (It will have been noticed that 1.16 is missing. This was no doubt a slip.)

With 2 Timothy 2 there is a closer relationship between sermons and commentary:

Commentary	Sermons	Number	
2.1-7	2.1-3	VIII	a.m.
	3-6	IX	p.m.
8-13	8-10	X	a.m.
	8-13	XI	p.m.
14-18	14-15	XII	p.m.
	16-18	XIII	a.m.
19-21	19	XIV	p.m.
	20-21	XV	a.m.
22-26	22-26	XVI	a.m.
	23-26	XVII	p.m.

Here vv. 1-7 serves for May 19 (with v. 7 omitted); vv. 8-13 come on May 26; he is then thrown out by the need for a Whit Sunday sermon on June 2 and has to take part of vv. 14-18 on the following Sunday morning. Thereafter he divides vv. 19-21 between two Sundays, does not preach on the afternoon of June 16 and so preaches in effect twice on vv. 22-26 on June 23.

It is not possible, for several reasons, to make a similar comparison for Old Testament sermons. We may assume, however, that he took the same care in the arrangement of sets; but he was certainly not able to arrange a weekly self-contained context.

We return to his treatment of the text. After the introductory matter of which we spoke he will announce the first clause or sentence he is going to expound. This (written in italics in the manuscripts) will nearly always differ somewhat in working from what he had originally given out as his text. Thus, two examples taken from Isa. 30-41. Isa. 30.1 as at first announced runs: '*Malheur sur les enfans pervers*' — 'Woe to the perverse children'. (ms. fr. 18 fol. 2ʳ). When this is repeated, '*pervers*' becomes '*rebelles et desobeissans*' — 'rebellious and disobedient' (ms. fr. 18 fol.3ᵛ). In Isa. 30.15, '*En repos, en repos vous serez sauvez, et en vous tenant quoys, et en silence sera vostre force*' ('In rest, in rest you will be saved, and in keeping yourselves quiet, and in silence will be your strength') (ms. fr. 18 fol. 26ʳ) becomes '*En repos et en vous tenant quois vous serez à seurté; et en repos et en silence sera vostre force*' (ms. fr. 18 fol. 28ᵛ) — 'In rest and in keeping yourselves quiet you will be in safety; and in rest and silence will be your strength'. Apart from the numerous occasions when the secondary text is put in the form of reported speech with the necessary alterations which that entails, the differences are due to either Calvin translating direct from the Hebrew and so giving a slightly different rendering or to his paraphrasing. If the latter, it will spring from an attempt to do justice to nuances in the Hebrew or to make the phrase or word easier to understand.

Having thus announced the secondary text, Calvin proceeds to expound it. Sometimes (but by no means always) he will explain the meaning, usually in simple and general terms. 'But, in order that this teaching may be the better understood, let us take the explanation that St Paul gives when he says that *avarice is the root of all evils*. When he speaks like this he does not mean that all the sins which men commit proceed from avarice — a glutton, a drunkard, or a lecher, a blasphemer, could well be free from this vice . . . So how is it that St Paul says that "avarice is the root of all evils"? He means . . . ' (1 Tim. 6.10. Sermon XLIX. CO 53.585[16-28]).

Occasionally he will explain the meaning of a word more carefully, but without ever (so far as I have noticed) giving the Hebrew or Greek original. At the most it will be 'the word that — uses is as much as to say . . .' Some of the old English translators burden the sermons with a trifle more learning than he himself proferred. Quite often Arthur Golding makes Calvin utter the word 'Hebrew'; as thus: 'The Hebrew word that Iob vseth, signifieth sometimes *to shet up*, and somtymes also *to ioyne or close together*' (*Sermons . . . vpon the Booke of Iob*, 450a[26-28]). In such cases all that we find in the French is (as here), 'This word which Job uses signifies . . .' (Job 26.9.

Sermon XCVI. CO 34.433[10-11]).

The same is true for the New Testament. He will never speak the original Greek word and will rarely refer to 'the Greek'. In the passage which follows, showing how he dealt with and simplified textual or exegetical difficulties, we may suspect that the word 'Greek' was added for the printed edition: 'But before all we must examine more carefully what St Paul meant by this word *profane vanity of babbling (vanité prophane de babil)*. For there are two Greek words very close to one another and apparently very similar — as far as pronunciation goes they seem the same. There was a difference of reading; some, instead of "*vanity*" put "*newness* of babbling". But the true and plain reading is "vanity". However, this word "vanity" means as good as "emptying" (*vuidange* = *vidange*), that there is only a futile appearance, no firmness' (Sermon LIV. 1 Tim. 6.20. CO 53.650[32-43]).

Just how far he has simplified it comes out in the same passage in the commentary on 1 Timothy: 'that they translate κενοφωνίας " emptiness of words" (*inanitates vocum*) is passable, except that they are afterwards led astray by the ambiguity and explain it wrongly — for they take "words" for individual words like "fate" or "fortune" (CO 52.335[15-19]). And later: 'The old translator, reading καινοφωνίας with a diphthong, translated it "newness". And it appears from old commentaries that this reading was at one time received by many; some Greek copies (*codices*) still keep it. But the former, which I have followed, fits far better' (CO 52.336[6-11]).

Having embarked on this subject, we may take the opportunity to point out the learning that lies, nearly always concealed, behind Calvin's deceptively simple explanations of his author's meaning. The comments on 1 Tim. 6.20 mention, first, anonymous translators who render καινοφωνίας as *inanitates vocum*. This is Erasmus' translation (in fact, transposed). His *Annotationes* (1535) seem also to supply the material for some other of Calvin's comments. We note that one of the Greek copies reading καινοφωνίας was Colinaeus (1534). The majority of the contemporary printed Greek New Testaments, including Stephanus (1550) and Complutensis (1522), agree with Erasmus here. When Calvin preached on the verse this textual and exegetical tradition was present in his mind; but there it stayed.

Veiled, also, are the other authors whom Calvin sometimes mentions. They become some such generalisations as '*aucuns*', 'some'. A typical example is furnished by Isa. 32.9: '*Voilà*, then, why the Prophet now says, "*You women who are at rest, raise yourselves, and you delicate daughters who are seated*, and who lounge in your ease and delights, you must raise yourselves". It is true that some take these two words, "women" and "daughters" as similes for "towns" and "villages", for Scripture often talks like that' (ms. fr. 18 fol. 108ᵛ-109ʳ). The editors supply the following foot-note: '*some*. Among Jewish exegetes, the Targum: "Raise yourselves, O provinces... O towns' (104-105); this is followed by Raschi (3.189) and Kimchi (246). Christian exegetes have either agreed with this (Cyril of Alexandria, PG 70.707-8; Luther, WA 25.211; Brenz — "For he calls rich women 'great cities' . . . And you daughters, that is, smaller towns and villages" (411)) or they will give the other meaning, of "synagogue" (Procopius PG 87.2281-2; Jerome, CC 73.409; *Glossa ordinaria*, 59 E; Münster: "The Jews by 'women' understand cities, and by 'daughters' lesser places like strong-holds, villages, etc." (*Biblia Hebraica* 2.389ʳ)'. The editors are not suggesting that Calvin had read all these authors in preparation for his sermon, but are only giving some indication of the exegetical tradition which lay behind his simple '*aucuns*'. (Very many more examples may be found in my translation and edition of the Sermons on Isa. 53.) The occasions when Calvin himself mentioned another author by name are rare indeed.

The meaning explained, he goes on to expound the sentence or clause. There is no careful separating out of different senses of Scripture (literal, moral, spiritual, etc.) in the manner of some patristic and medieval preachers, for Calvin was not a slave to any theory of Biblical interpretation. Each place is treated on its merits; but above all, the question he has asked himself in preparation is 'How is this profitable to the congregation?' And therefore every part of every passage is addressed directly to that congregation. Historical relativising has no place and therefore there is no re-interpretation of Scripture

— that pseudo-scholarly method whereby the author is made to say something 'relevant' (that is, something the preacher would prefer him so say). The solution of the problem about the contemporaneity of the Biblical message Calvin left to the Holy Spirit, to whom it properly belongs. When he had understood it himself as a sixteenth century man and had put it in the sixteenth century form of sixteenth century French for his sixteenth century congregation there was really nothing more for him to do but to trust to the Holy Spirit who was the same in the sixteenth century A.D. that he had been in the sixteenth century B.C. We may put it another way and say that Calvin believed in the universal relevance of Holy Scripture. There was not a man, woman, or child in the congregation to whom each book and each passage did not apply. It was just a question of trying his best to bring it home to them.

The application is usually direct and immediate. Sometimes the Scriptural passage is specifically related to a person or a situation or is addressed to a class of persons. Thus in Sermon III on 2 Tim. (1-6): 'He adds, *See that you do still better.* He does not say, "It is enough; I let you off; I free you;" but "You must complete it. Seeing you have borne yourself valiantly, realize how much you are bound to God who has been so gracious to you. For he does not want to be served by us for three days — it is for life and death. So then, continue and do not give up in mid-course". *Voilà* what St Paul meant. Do we, then, wish to correct the coldness and laziness that is in us? . . .' (CO 54.31[29-39]). What is true of Timothy, is true of "us" also.

Or again on Deut. 1.19ff. ('Then we departed from Horeb and went through the great and terrible wilderness . . . and we came to Kadesh-Barnea. And I said unto you, "Ye are come unto the mountain of the Amorites, which the Lord our God doth give us . . .")'. This, says Calvin, is a rebuke to the Jews for their ingratitude for the many blessings God had given them. They ought never to have forgotten how he brought them safely through the terrible desert. Their own eyes had seen it. Moses had explained it to them. "'Know, then, your ingratitude, when you have refused to enter into the inheritance which God promised to your fathers and which he had ready for you". Now nevertheless, *we* have to gather here in the first place a good doctrine; it is that, seeing that God has already declared to *us* his goodness in making his blessing felt, *we* are so much the more to be condemned if *we* do not rest entirely in him and do not put *our* trust in him, to walk boldly and without doubtings' (CO 25.651[23-32]). This should not be interpreted, *tout court*, as an employment of the tropological sense. The children of Israel and the children of Geneva were brothers under the skin, for all their different clothes and different languages and different manners. But especially it is that 'whatsoever things were written aforetime were written for our learning' (Rom. 15.4).

Or again, what is applicable to one class is also to be extended to all the congregation. On 1 Tim. 1.12. ('I thank Christ Jesus our Lord, who hath enabled me, for that he counted me faithful, putting me into the ministry, who was before a blasphemer and a persecutor, and injurious; but I obtained mercy...'). This is first expounded of St Paul himself. Next, 'It remains now that we draw profit from this teaching. And in the first place let us note well that to preach the Word of God is no small or cheap thing' (CO 53.67[13-17]). He expounds it accordingly of preachers, ending, '*Voilà* how ministers of the Word of God ought to apply this doctrine to their use' (CO 53.68[16-18]). But then, 'Nevertheless, it is also useful for all the people' (CO 53.68[19-20]).

Thus, clause by clause, verse by verse, the congregation was led through the epistle or the prophecy or the narrative. From one aspect the Bible was teaching, from another it was a mirror, from another it was a commination, from another a consolation. The multifarious strands of the Biblical message run through Calvin's sermons in all their rich profusion. The book of Job presents a very different picture from the Pastoral Epistles. Isaiah, Jeremiah, Ezekiel, Micah are all Hebrew prophets but each has his own individual climate and thought world.

The variety is mirrored in Calvin's sermons on all these books. For six months, or a year, or more, he and his congregation will become steeped in the thought of an author. See how this would be with the sets of sermons with which we are especially interested in this book. From September 1554 until August 1555 the message of 1 and 2 Timothy is taught twice a

Sunday. Not only are most of the distinctively Pauline doctrines given expression — salvation through Christ alone, predestination, faith, grace, perseverance, holiness, love — but also and perhaps above all, the place of preaching in the order of salvation. All this the congregation will be hearing on Sunday. But during the week they will be transported to the drama of suffering Job and his friends, to the rule of God over Satan. And now the message will be that God orders all things in heaven and earth and we must rely on him and trust in him whatever may happen in the world or to us personally. All will be well, for God is in command. Job being concluded while 1 Timothy is still continuing, Deuteronomy becomes the book for the week-days. Now the emphasis moves from providence and theodicy and trust to the learning of God's will in the Law. Now the distinctiveness from 1 and 2 Timothy is less marked; in the Pastorals and in Deuteronomy teaching or preaching plays a major part; in them both, grace, faith and righteousness predominate. There is still the difference in age and understanding between Moses and Paul, above all, the difference between the time before and the time after the Sun of righteousness had risen. Yet the Law, the second giving of which is recorded in Deuteronomy, is the subject of the New Testament preaching. We remember that Calvin said that the Apostles did nothing but interpret the Law as having been fulfilled in Jesus Christ. Nevertheless, while on Sundays St Pierre heard of Christ Jesus the end of the Law, on weekdays it heard the message of the Law itself which was to be fulfilled in Christ.

This 'before' and 'since' demanded a somewhat different manner of treatment. In his Old Testament commentaries Calvin set out to expound the authors in their particular situation of living before the Incarnation and therefore of being ignorant of the fulfilment of what they were looking forward to. He did not inject into their thinking the complete Gospel of the New Testament, but interpreted them according to the measure of light they had been given. Traditionally messianic passages were expounded Messianically, that is, of Christ and his Gospel. Certain persons or institutions were interpreted as 'types' of Christ. He also uses New Testament language in his explanations and has no hesitations about turning to New Testament authors for confirmation. But he is always careful to treat the authors in their historical context of living before the Incarnation.

The same thing is only partly true for the sermons on the Old Testament. He keeps to the historical context in the interpretation and exegesis of passages. For this reason there may be little or no mention of Jesus Christ or the Gospel in a sermon. When, however, he comes to the application of passages, the situation is at once different. 'We', to whom he is speaking, do not live before the Incarnation and the witness of the New Testament and it would be artificial and foolish to try to carry over the superseded historical conditions. So now he is free to speak in a Christian way to Christian people.

A remarkable and perhaps rather amusing example occurs in Sermon CLII on Job. The text is Job 39.16-17, which Calvin paraphrases and condenses as 'God has left destitute the wisdom of the ostrich'. 'Let us know that this is to teach us that we have reason and judgment. . . . For what is it to judge between good and evil and to know what our duty is, not only for walking in this world but for aspiring to the heavenly life? What is it that we should know that God has formed us to his image and that he has prepared for us our inheritance on high? So when we have that judgment of being able to distinguish between honesty and villainy, between vice and virtue, and moreover when God enlightens us by his Holy Spirit, so that the heavens are, as it were, open to us and we pass above the world to come to the company of the Angels, to the immortal glory which was won for us by our Lord Jesus Christ — when, I say, we have that, how greatly we should magnify such a treasure! (CO 35.424^{51}-425^{14}). We have travelled far from the land of Uz. But there is no other mention of Christ in all the sermon, which is devoted to the lessons to be learned from elephants and peacocks, wild asses and unicorns, snails and storks. Calvin has undertaken to expound Job and this he will do, whatever comes up. The Book of Job is a highly individual work; but we shall find that Calvin pursues the same course in all his Old Testament sermons of interpreting according to the historical context but applying within the context of the Christian Faith.

Chapter 10

The Message of Scripture

The previous chapter ended on the note of variety. But for Calvin as for all previous Christian theologians, Holy Scripture was a unity. They did not all understand or explain that unity in the same way, but it was accepted by them all as a principle of Bible study. Hence it was not the variety of Scripture with which Calvin was chiefly concerned but the unity. The variety, after all, took care of itself, so long as the context was always faithfully observed. The unity, however, meant that one single message was being declared, whether the sermon was on Daniel or Deuteronomy, Micah or Galatians.

Holy Scripture is a unity because its one author is the Holy Spirit, who remains constant to himself. Its message is one because it is God's one Word or message to mankind. At this point we go on to ask after the nature of that message according to Calvin. He will often call it 'the Faith'. This is summed up in the historic creed. So in the 1536 *Institutio* he will say, 'It now remains to ask the nature of the Faith. What it is we may easily learn from the so-called Apostolic Symbol, in which is briefly collected a compendium and as it were epitome of the Faith in which the Catholic Church agrees' (OS 1.68). But the Creed itself and thus also the Faith is in its turn 'a compendium and as it were epitome' of the teaching of Scripture taken as a whole.

We do not, in fact, find Calvin directly applying the Creed to his text — or, at least, he does not do this as a deliberate policy of interpretation; he may do it occasionally by way of illustration. What he does, however, is frequently to give the congregation a summary of the Biblical message, or of 'doctrine', or of the Gospel, or of the Faith — the terms are as good as synonymous in this context. The Pastoral Epistles, with their instructions on the work of the ministry and their demand for 'sound teaching', prompt him on occasion to affirm the character of that sound teaching — that is, the essential message of the Bible.

The first example occurs in Sermon III of 1 Timothy. The text is 1.5: 'the end of the commandment is love out of . . . faith unfeigned'. Calvin's introductory remark shows us that what is to follow is a summary of 'true doctrine' or 'the Faith': 'St Paul sets down as it were the fount of true doctrine, that we may be instructed in the Faith' (CO 53.31[9-11]). He summarizes this as:

1. that we may know what our God is like;
2. that we may know by experience that he is our Father;
3. that we may rest in him entirely;
4. that we call upon him boldly;
5. that we shall have no doubt that he will hear us;
6. that he wishes to help us in our need;
7. and that we await the eternal salvation he has promised us. (CO 53.31[11-17]).

But he immediately enlarges on this: 'See then what the Faith is of which St Paul speaks; it is, in fact:'

1. that we may be assured what our God is like;
2. that we adore him;
3. that none constructs idols in his head;
4. that we have not a God invented at random;
5. that we may know that the living God has revealed himself to us;
6. and has adopted us by his free goodness.

And why has God done this?

7. in order that we can have recourse to him entirely;
8. and that we may not doubt that we are his children and shall be heirs of his kingdom.

Now, by what means can we obtain the privilege of being able

9. to call God our Father boldly;
10. and come familiarly to him?
11. Because our sins are pardoned in the name of our Lord Jesus Christ;
12. and when we are members of God's only Son,

13. God holds us as his children.

He concludes: 'So, then, our faith must look to our Lord Jesus Christ and our view must be fastened entirely on him, or else we cannot approach God his Father — for in ourselves we are too far away. All that, as I have said, is contained in the law' (CO 53.31[18-42]). Note, 'the Law'; this Faith is the message of the Old Testament.

Our second example comes in Sermon XLVII of 1 Timothy. The text is 6.3: 'If any man teach otherwise and consent not . . . to the doctrine which is according to godliness'. Calvin's brief introduction runs: 'See, then, what is the sum of the pure doctrine which ought to be preached daily and to which one ought to keep' (CO 53.557[34-36]):

1. that we know there is nothing in us but complete poverty and wretchedness;
2. and therefore that we seek God;
3. and that by the way and in the direction he has given us;
4. and this is in the person of our Lord Jesus Christ. It is necessary, then,
5. that we grasp the grace he has given;
6. so that, being members of our Lord Jesus Christ by faith,
7. we may not doubt that he leads us to God his Father and consequently to the kingdom of heaven.

Now, all this presupposes that we receive from Christ what we lack, since in us there is nothing but complete poverty. It is necessary, then,

8. that we be enriched with the blessings which Jesus Christ has brought us and gives us,
9. so that we may be bold to call upon God and have recourse to him.

And meanwhile

10. that we undertake to rule our life fittingly;
11. and that none shall invent his own devotions (CO 53.557[36]-558[2]).

The third example occurs in Sermon VI on 2 Timothy. The text is 1.13: 'hold the pattern of sound words'.

'Now, the Faith [or, faith] is:'
1. to know what the true God is (so that we are not diverted by our imaginings or drawn to idolatry);
2. to know the living God;

3. to know him as our Father;
4. so that we can rest entirely in him and put our trust in him;
5. that we call upon him boldly, not doubting that our requests will be heard (CO 54.71$^{2\text{-}13}$).

Again he adds a repetition: 'See, then, what faith [or, Faith] means':

1. that we know what the true God is;
2. that we hold him as our Father and Saviour;
3. that we are assured of his grace and love;
4. that in true trust we call upon him;
5. And then, that if we have *la Charité*, we shall be pure and irreproachable before God;
6. And this in Christ Jesus (CO 54.71$^{19\text{-}54}$).

Sermon XII of *2 Timothy* furnishes us with our fourth example. The text is 2.14: 'that they strive not about words'. 'Let us hold to the simplicity of the Gospel. Let us keep to it entirely. And we shall be taught':[1]

1. that we have a God who declares himself to be Father and Saviour to us;
2. that we may know the means by which we find grace before him — in the name of our Lord Jesus Christ;
3. that we know his will;
4. that we know how and with what boldness we ought to call on him;
5. that we know how he draws us to himself;
6. that we 'meditate' his promises;
7. and that we conjoin the Sacraments as 'the second signature';
8. that we know that all this proceeds from God's free goodness and from his being pleased to join us with himself;
9. hoping that he will lead us to the end (CO 54.144^{43}-145^3).

Before we attempt to make a synthesis of these four summaries of the Faith, we shall do well to look at the spirit they show. And the first thing that must strike any reader is their almost entirely positive character. Everything said about God is positive. About man the only negative statements are of his 'poverty

---

[1] For the sake of easy transitions I have paraphrased here. Calvin in fact said, 'And when we shall have been taught'.

and wretchedness' and the prohibitions of idolatry. Even these are, so to say, stepping stones, the first to riches, the second to the knowledge of the true God. The second equally obvious point is that in fact only one subject is being treated throughout — God as he gives himself to be known by us in Jesus Christ. All that is said about man not only depends on this one subject but is also, strictly speaking, a part of it. These two characteristics cast a glow of happiness and confidence and hopefulness over the whole. The Gospel, the doctrine, the Faith, is for Calvin indeed *eu-angellion*, the good tidings of great joy.

As we examine the summaries in detail we see that Calvin dwells, in regard to God, on two concepts; first, on what God is like — *quel est nostre Dieu*, 'what is our God [like]', a phrase repeated several times. This is the equivalent in the sermons of the point he makes in the *Institutio* and elsewhere, that it is useless to play the game of speculating on the essence of God, *quid sit Deus*, 'what God is'; for what concerns us is to learn of his inward and outward attitude towards us, *qualis sit Deus*, 'of what character God is' (*Inst*.I.ii.2). Calvin's French translation uses the same phrase that we have in the sermon: 'rather it behoves us to know *quel il est*' (*Institution* ed. J.-D. Benoît I.p.56). Everything else that the summaries say about God falls under this heading and expounds, so to say, God's inward and outward attitude (i.e. will) towards us.

Quel est nostre Dieu? Quel est le vray Dieu? First, he is the one who reveals himself; an assertion which comes in all the summaries. He has revealed himself as the living God; he has been pleased to communicate himself to us; God is the God who declares himself. On this depends the truth of the rest of the statements about God as well as the validity of the various parts of our actions towards God. For on the one hand the truth of any statement about God depends on self-disclosure by God, who alone has knowledge of himself, and on the other hand, the validity of our belief, trust, worship, praying, etc. depend on the truth of what is believed, trusted, etc.

Secondly, God reveals himself as the one who wishes to help us in our need, who gives us grace, who shows his free goodness, who shows his grace and love, who lets us come familiarly to him and listens to our prayers. It is a remarkable fact that not a word occurs in the summaries about God's wrath, judgment, or rejection. All is positive and joyful — grace, goodness, love, a God who wishes to help.

And thirdly, in accord with this, God reveals himself to us as Father, as the one who adopts us to be his children, who makes us heirs of his kingdom, who joins us with himself; who reveals himself as Saviour, pardoning our sins, enriching us with blessings, who gives us the hope of eternal salvation.

God has revealed himself in this positive, loving manner. It would appear, then, that this part of our exposition is ended and we can now go on to the implications for ourselves. But in fact the definite word has not yet been spoken. The truth and the positiveness of the revelation, indeed the very revelation itself, depend upon the means of revelation. As we look at each of the summaries we see that, either at the beginning or at some point along the way, revelation becomes the person of Jesus Christ.

Thus, in the repetition of the first summary, Calvin asks how we can obtain the privilege of being able to call God our Father and come to him. And his reply is, 'Because our sins are pardoned in the name of our Lord Jesus Christ, and when we are members of his only Son, we can be sure that God regards us and confesses us as his children' (CO 53.31[32-36]).

The sum of pure doctrine is given in the second in Christological categories throughout. We are poor and wretched; if we are to seek God it must be 'by the way and in the direction he has given us', that is, in the person of our Lord Jesus Christ. It is therefore necessary for us to lay hold on the grace he has given and, as members by faith of our Lord Jesus Christ, not to doubt that he is the way to God his Father. In ourselves we are poor absolutely, but 'we are enriched with the blessings which Jesus Christ has brought us and which he gives us' (CO 53 557[51-53]).

The third summary seems to contain no reference to Christ. But in fact what happens is that Calvin is following the clauses of his text and arrives later with St Paul at the last clause, 'which is in Christ Jesus'. Hence all that he has placed in this summary is made dependent on Christ: 'Now, especially St Paul adds that it is *in Jesus Christ,* in order that we may have the

Lord Jesus for our guide and conductor if we wish to be instructed and built up both in charity and in the Faith [or, in faith]. And it is impossible for us to have faith before we have known Jesus Christ' (CO 54.71$^{49\text{-}54}$).

The fourth summary, like the second, brings Christ forward immediately. The way in which we know that God is gracious to us and declares himself to be our Father and Saviour is 'in the name of our Lord Jesus Christ'. It is through him that we know God's will and that he draws us to himself.

It is plain to see why Calvin will say: 'So, then, our faith must look to our Lord Jesus Christ and our gaze must be fastened entirely on him, or else we cannot approach God his Father — for in ourselves we are too far away' (CO 53.31$^{36\text{-}41}$).

Much of what concerns man, to whom God has revealed himself and given his grace, has already been stated. We are God's children, we are heirs of his kingdom, we are members of Christ, God draws us to himself, and so on. But these summaries of 'true doctrine' or the Gospel, or what we have called the essential message of the Bible, also embrace our side in this relationship. Certainly, this 'our side' is in no degree independent; it is possible, set in motion, and brought to its conclusion by 'God's side'.

This appears clearly in the way that each summary takes its start from our knowledge of God (a knowledge of both mind and heart) which corresponds to the truth of God revealed in Holy Scripture. From this flows all that is said about 'our side'. Thus, the first opens with 'And what does this word mean except that *we know what our God is like*' (expressed in the repetition as '*that we may be assured what our God is like*'). And then, knowing what our God is like — that is, our Father — we can rest in him, call upon him, and await our salvation. The other examples are expressed rather differently, in terms dictated by the particular Biblical text expounded: but they observe the same pattern of the relationship.

'Our knowledge of God' means in these summaries knowledge of God in Christ; knowledge that is belief and trust, obedience and love, adoration and hope. It is the words 'in Christ' which are definitive here. We have no knowledge of God as Father and Saviour apart from him. Our belief and trust in Christ is our belief and trust in God. Our obedience, love, and adoration are directed towards God in Christ. And he is our hope. All this is expressed, most of it explicitly, in the summaries. But the all-embracing statement is that we are 'members of Christ': 'when we are members of the only Son we can conclude that God holds us and avows us for his children' (CO 53.31$^{34\text{-}36}$); 'being members of our Lord Jesus Christ, we may not doubt that he leads us to God his Father' (CO 53.557$^{46\text{-}48}$). Because Christ has made himself one with us and us one with himself, we share in his knowledge of God, and are enriched by the blessings which he has won and enjoys.

Corresponding, then, to the summaries of God's revelation of himself in Holy Scripture we have summaries of God's revelation of ourselves in Holy Scripture. It is the revelation of our sin and idolatry and of our pardon through Christ. It is the revelation of how we are 'drawn' to God by and in Jesus Christ, of how we are children of God and heirs of his kingdom. It tells us that we may rest in God, that we may have recourse to God and call on him boldly (notice how often 'boldly' comes), that we need have no doubt of his responding. And finally, it lays before us a life ruled according to God's will, a life of '*charité*' lived in the hope of God's promises, lived in the strength of God's Word and of the 'second signature', the Sacraments.

There is one aspect of the summaries of the Faith which so far we have barely mentioned but which does, in fact, inform all the rest. In the first it appears, as, 'and that we await the eternal salvation he has promised us' (CO 53.31$^{16\text{-}17}$) and 'that we may not doubt that ... we shall be heirs of his kingdom (CO 53.31$^{27\text{-}28}$). In the second it is, 'we may not doubt that he leads us to God his Father and consequently to the kingdom of heaven' (CO 53.557$^{47\text{-}49}$). Our third summary is lacking in this regard. The fourth ends with, 'hoping that he will lead us even to the end' (CO 54.145^3) and then a few lines later, 'contemplating the immortal glory that he promises us' (CO 54.145$^{21\text{-}22}$).

The teaching of the sermons is eschatological, not in the sense that at certain points, depending on the text, heaven and eternal life are mentioned, but in that everything is viewed in

The Message of Scripture

the light of the eternal inheritance. This gives them an extraordinarily hopeful and positive quality, outweighing any of the darker aspects. It is probably true to say that every sermon ends on a positive and joyful note.

Here, then, are some of Calvin's summaries of the essential message of the Bible. Besides these, he also sometimes gave summaries of what was daily preached in Geneva. But these also, since it was intended that only pure (i.e. Biblical) doctrine should be preached, are indications of Calvin's view of the essential message of Scripture. One of the most comprehensive occurs in Sermon VII on 1 Corinthians. The text is 10.15: 'I speak to men of understanding':

'As often as we come to the sermon we are taught of the free promises of God, to show us that it is entirely in his goodness and mercy that we must rest; that we must not be grounded on our merits or on anything that we bring from our side; but it is necessary for God to stretch out his hand to us, to begin and accomplish all. And that (as Scripture shows us) is applied to us by our Lord Jesus Christ, so that we must seek him entirely ... and that we must know that Jesus Christ alone must lead us. That, I say, is shown us every day. It is also declared to us that the service of God does not consist in imagining foolish devotions ... but we must serve God in obedience. After that, we are shown that in the first place we must make a sacrifice of our hearts and affections to him, and that hypocrisy is detestable to him. All that is declared to us daily. After that, we are shown how we can call upon God; we are shown by what tokens we have been baptized and what is the fruit of our Baptism for our whole lives, even to our death; why it is that the Lord's Supper is administered. All that is declared to us' (CO 49. 661[18-47]).

The common message of Scripture expressed in these summaries becomes in its turn the way in which all the Bible is to be understood, for it generates a certain hermeneutical point of view or attitude. The quintessence of the teaching 'declared to us daily' is that the hidden God reveals himself and that men are thereby brought out of darkness into light. Consequently, the teachers of the Church shall be content with God's self-revelation, not wishing for or attempting some other way to the knowledge of God, and not desiring to know more than God vouchsafes to bestow. Sermon XXII on Deuteronomy (4.11, according to Calvin's rendering of the verse, 'he spoke from the midst of the fire. And nevertheless there was a great cloud, there was darkness and obscurity'): 'God does not wish to be unknown by men, but he wishes to reveal himself in such a way that we know how to distinguish between him and the idols that have been made, that we hold him for our Father, that we know that we have been called to the knowledge of his truth, and how we can come to him in complete boldness to call upon him and to have our refuge in him. *Voilà*, then, how God wished to reveal himself to the people of Israel, when the Law was published. And *voilà* how he continues still today. But nevertheless, the cloud is before their eyes, so that men may know their ignorance. And then, seeing we are too extravagant and want to know twice as much as is permitted, even to know what is impossible for us, this is why God put between himself and the people a great, dense cloud. If we are really convinced of that, it will be like a key to give us understanding of all Holy Scripture. And why? Because when we come to read or to hear we shall be assured that our Lord is not mocking when he speaks like this . . . See how we would profit if we had this well printed in our heart, that God reveals himself to us so far as is useful for our salvation. And moreover we would adore in complete simplicity what we do not understand; each one would walk according to the portion of his faith; we would always try to approach him and to be strengthened' (CO 26.140[45]-141[24]).

What Calvin has in mind here by 'a key to give us understanding of all Holy Scripture' is not some doctrinal principle which can be employed universally as an aid to interpretation but rather a point of view, a way of looking at the Bible, in whole or in its parts. It is something ingrained — 'if we are really convinced of that': 'if we had this well printed in our heart' — and therefore does not have to be continually sought from without in order to be applied. But it is not a point of view that we have reached by our own thinking. On the contrary, it is the essential message of Holy Scripture, the summary or abstract of the teaching of the Old and New Testaments. That which is true of the whole is true of the parts. Therefore the parts are to be understood according to the whole. This is a general literary dictum, valid for the understanding of any consistent and coherent document. When applied to Holy Scripture it is based on belief in the unity and truth of Scripture and is thereby strengthened.

This point of view, then, this way of reading the Bible, is the belief that God, otherwise unknown, is graciously pleased to reveal himself, and that for our salvation. Besides being a point of view it is an attitude of heart, of being content with God's self-revelation.

Earlier we spoke of the expository preacher as a chameleon, taking his colour from that of the passage on which he was alighted. This is certainly true of Calvin, with his outstanding gift of entering into the mind of his author. If exposition consists in explaining the meaning of the passage, we should expect sermons on 1 Tim. 1.15 ('Christ Jesus came into the world to save sinners of whom I am chief'), Deut. 3.12 ('and half mount Gilead, and the cities thereof, gave I unto the Reubenites and the Gadites'), and Job 26.7 ('He stretcheth out the north over the empty place, and hangeth the earth upon nothing') to differ as widely from one another as do the texts themselves. Let us see what happens when Calvin treats of these three places.

Sermon VII on 1 Timothy covers vv. 13b-15 of Chapter 1. It is therefore within this context of St Paul's confession that he, formerly a blasphemer and persecutor, had obtained mercy from God, whose grace had abounded more and more; 'Christ Jesus came into the world to save sinners, of whom I am chief'. This, says Calvin when he reaches the verse about half-way through his sermon, declares what a great miracle God wrought when he converted Paul. But St Paul himself broadens the scope of the confession to make it 'a general teaching for all God's children, so that in his person we may be the more assured of our salvation and of the remission of our sins' (CO 53.82$^{53\text{-}55}$).

From this point Calvin concentrates upon the latter part of the verse, 'sinners, of whom I am chief'. St Paul humbled himself in this confession, in order that God's glory might be the better known. And this is a general truth; God is never exalted as he deserves to be unless we are completely '*confuz et abysmez*', ashamed and overwhelmed. Rom. 3.23 says this clearly enough; God's glory appears only when every mouth is stopped and we realize how heavily we are in debt to him. The coverings that men use to hide their sins are like clouds obscuring the glory of God.

This is the burden of the sermon until its calmly triumphant close: 'After he had made such a confession of his sins as we have heard, "Oh", says he, "let glory and honour be rendered to God alone, who is immortal and invisible, who is our King eternal". When St Paul speaks like this, he shows that he cannot be satisfied with such a declaration of the graces that he has received from God — as if he said that he was in the depths of death and God had drawn him out. So when we think of the goodness and mercy of God and of the miserable state in which we were before he made us feel his grace, we shall be stirred to make confession of our sins; yes, in truth, because God will be witness — so that we shall not fear to pronounce it before him, before his Angels, and before all creatures' (CO 53.88[35-50]).

Deut. 7.12 comes in Sermon XVI, preached on Wednesday, May 8, 1555. The full text was Chapter 7.12-22 and Calvin's rendering of v. 12b was 'he [Moses] had given that region to the sons of Reuben and to the sons of Gad — that is to say, to their line'. He first explains the circumstances of this gift according to Num. 32.1-33. The two tribes had asked for this particular piece of country as especially suited to their trade as cattle-men. In response to Moses' indignation at their not helping the other tribes in their conquest of the promised land they proposed to leave their cattle and their families in this region and themselves to go over Jordan and fight alongside the other tribes. 'Now, in this,' says Calvin, 'we have to observe the goodness of God. For if he had not been the protector of what remained in that country, what would have happened? There were women, there were little children, left with the cattle. Now, we know that all their neighbours wanted only to destroy the people of Israel, that everywhere hatred was stirred up — like a fire kindled. If, then, the children and the women had not been preserved under the hand of God and under his protection, would they not a hundred times have perished? Yet being now abandoned they have not been molested at all. Herein, then, the people ought to recognise in everything and everywhere the grace of God . . . *Voilà* what is Moses' intention in this passage' (CO 26.63^{41}-64^4).

The next sentence transports the story, or rather, its significance, from the dim past of patriarchal history to Wednesday, May 8, 1555: 'But today we can certainly also apply this message (*ceste doctrine*) to our instruction' (CO 26.64$^{4-5}$). If God so preserved the defenceless women and children, surrounded by powerful enemies, then we may know that our safety does not lie in being well-armed with human weapons. 'When we have neither walls nor ramparts, when we have nothing to uphold us — if we are under the command (*en la conduite*) of our God and he has the charge of our salvation, we have enough; we can defy our enemies . . . Let us learn, then, to call upon our God and to put ourselves into his hands. And seeing that he says that he will receive the poor and afflicted ones, that those who are destitute of all aid, who are not supported by the world, he promises to receive them, [*sic!*] let us go to him, being assured that the door will never be shut on us. Have we come to him? let us trust boldly that he will uphold us, and although we may be surrounded on all sides by enemies and it seems that we cannot escape out of their hands, God will be for us, to preserve us, even though in ourselves we are completely weak. *Voilà* what we have to remember from this example' (CO 26.64$^{12-34}$).

There is more to follow, however. Moses was blaming the Reubenites and Gadites for acting too hastily and for trying to settle in that country. They ought to have kept themselves under God's providence and not attempted anything on their own. 'So then, as we have seen previously, if we want God to bless us we must keep ourselves in the simplicity of his Word, attempt nothing whatever, not walk one step forward without his approval and not swerve either to the right or to the left' (CO 26.64$^{44-50}$).

This leads to a further point. The region chosen by the Reubenites and Gadites was desirable and fertile. They would have done better to have joined with their brethren rather than be cut off from the line of Judah. They were at ease in a fertile and rich land — and there was nothing but pride and rebellion in them. 'Let us learn, then, not to be so very ready to seek our own convenience and comfort and not to rush in and take control of this or that according to our own desires; but let us await the blessing of God' (CO 26.65[21-25]). Lot chose to live in Sodom, 'an earthly paradise'; but our Lord made him pay dearly for it. Although he was one of God's elect and although God had pity on him in the end and 'made him feel his grace', yet Lot was chastised as he deserved, for thinking too much of his own ease and profit. But in a flash Lot has vanished; one sentence he was there, the next it is 'us': 'By that we are taught to curb our desires, and when we see some advantage according to the flesh not to wish for it overmuch. If God gives it to us, let us accept it; but let us guard against being too eager in our desires — as our custom has been' (CO 26.65[37-43]).

With Job 26.7 we seem at first to be in another world again. The exposition of this verse comes at the end of Sermon XCV, the whole text being vv. 1-7. Calvin's rendering is, 'He stretches out the side of the north (*le costé de la Bise*) upon a waste place, and the earth is founded on nothing'. By speaking of 'the side of the north', says Calvin, Job means in fact the whole sky, because the sky turns round the pole, which is there. Just as in the wheels of a waggon you have the axle in the middle and the wheels, having a hole in the middle, turn around it, so with the sky: 'One sees that clearly — that is to say, those who best understand the movement of the firmament see — that the sky turns like this. For on the north side there is a star (which one sees with the eye) that is like this axle at the centre of a wheel, and one sees the firmament turning in the middle. There is another one which is hidden from us, which we cannot perceive, which is called "The Antarctit Pole". Why? Because the sky turns round it as well, as if there were an axle on which the wheel was set, as has been said. When I speak of the movement of the sky, I do not mean the sort of movement of the sun which we see every day; for the sun has a special movement of its own. But this is a universal movement for the whole firmament of heaven. Now, those two stars are, as it were, fixed (*attachées*); they neither move nor stray' (CO 34.430[4-20]).

After this lesson in astronomy comes the exposition. Why did Job speak like this? Because it is a miracle which should 'ravish us in amazement', even if it is a fact of experience. For it shows us 'that there is such a wisdom in God that we have to confess that it transcends all human senses and we can only adore this greatness of our God who has so declared himself in the creation of the world' (CO 34.430[27-31]).

The following day he pursued the theme even more fully, preaching on Job 26.8-14.

In these three examples we see a variety as wide as the texts that are expounded. Were further examples to be taken we should find further variety. Yet also the same central message. For although Calvin has betrayed to us his own predilections — his pleasure in unravelling the significance of a story, his interest in the physical sciences and so on — these subsidiary concerns do not take charge. They arise out of the text; they are expounded; they are left behind. Through all the variety occasioned by the variety of the texts there runs the Biblical point of view — the hidden God reveals himself for man's eternal and temporal good. It is this that governs Calvin's interpretation and application of his texts. In each of our examples we saw God in his gracious activity. In the first (1 Tim. 1.15) he wrought the miracle of Paul's conversion and drew him out of the depths of death; he is the Father, the Saviour, the forgiver of sins; he is good and merciful and makes us feel his grace; and although the context demands the stressing of sin, it is that glory and honour should be rendered to the King eternal, the immortal and invisible God. In the second (Deut. 7.12) God appears as the protector of the helpless, the women and children; we ought to trust God and commit ourselves to his charge; but that also means, putting ourselves under his command, to do only what he enjoins; moreover, being content to await God's gifts instead of snatching at them. In the third (Job 26.7) God is the one who has spoken by creating the world; his wisdom and his greatness compel us to amazement and adoration.

But within each of these distinctive expositions beats the heart of the Bible message — the gracious self-revelation of the hidden God and man's grateful acceptance and submission to it.

1. First page of manuscript of the Sermon on Isa. 30.28-33, showing the caligraphy of the preliminary material and first line, and the running hand of the sermon itself.

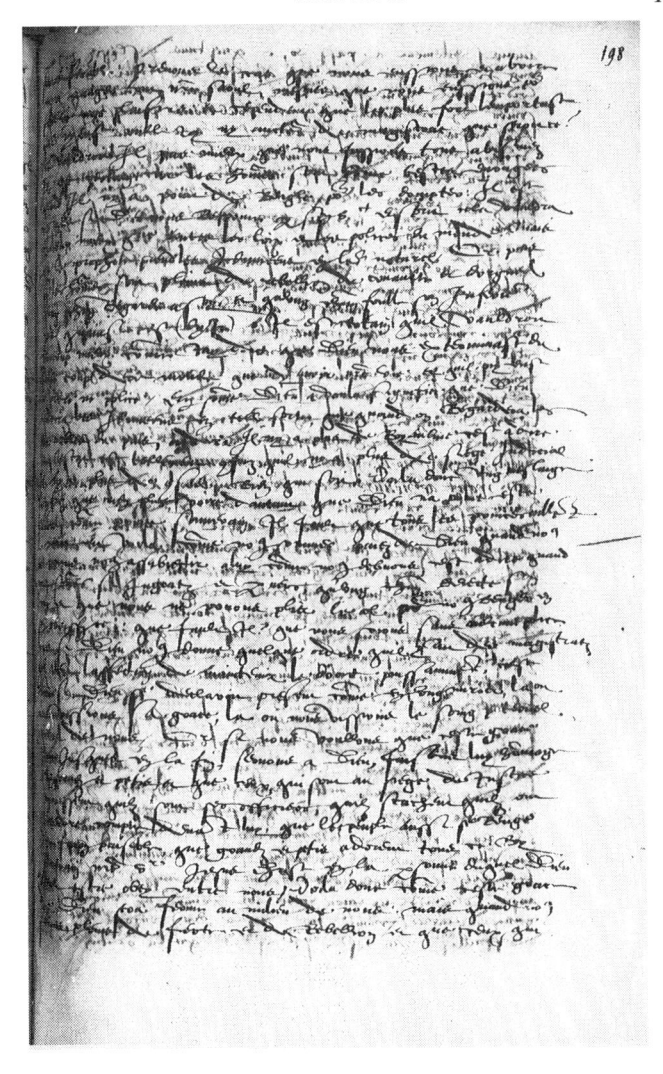

2. *A page of manuscript, illustrating why the editors of Corpus Reformatorum were put off from including the manuscript sermons in their edition. This is by no means the worst of the manuscripts, however. It is at least legible with care.*

3. One of the better pages of manuscript.

4. *Title page of the first edition of the* Sermons on the Pastoral Epistles.

**Certaine homi-
lies of. m. Ioan Calui
ne, conteining profitable and
necessarie, admonitiõ for this time,
with an Apologie of
Robert Horn.**

*Imprited at Rome, before the castle of .S. Angel,
at the signe of .S. Peter. Anno.
M. D. Liij.*

5. *Title page of the earliest English translation.*

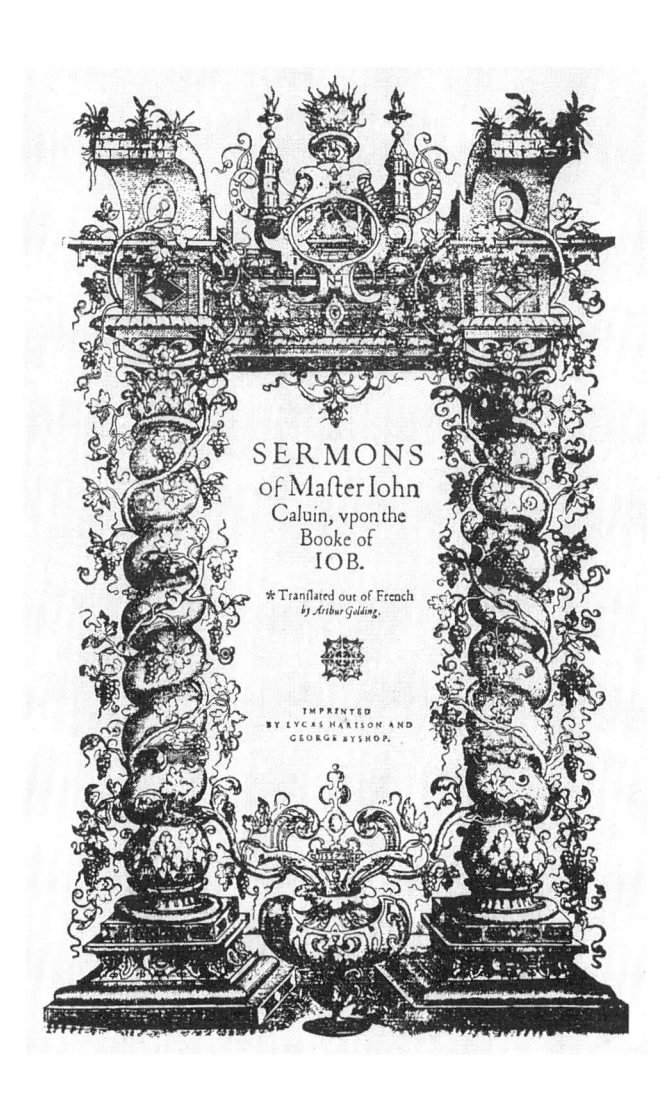

6. *Title page of the first edition of the English translation of the Sermons on Job.*

Chapter 11

The Stimuli of Exhortations

It has been clear that, in one way or another, Calvin set out to apply the substance of his texts to the congregation. We have tried to show how he did this in regard to teaching the Faith of the Bible. Now we go on to what he called in the Commentary on 2 Timothy (3.16-17) *institutio formandae vitae*— 'instruction on the framing of one's life'. Teaching by itself, or mere pointing out the way, is insufficient. There are needed also *stimuli exhortationum et reprehensionum*— 'the stimuli, or goads, of exhortations and reproofs'. St Paul's final clause, 'training in righteousness' is explained as showing 'the way to live a godly and holy life' (CO 52.384[4-12]).

We remind ourselves that the purpose of preaching is *édification*, the building up of the believer and the Church. More concretely, that the believer should increase in faith and the knowledge of God, in hope and love, putting to death his own wishes and desires, until after this life he shall be perfectly formed to the image of Christ. And also that the Church should more and more approximate on earth to what it is in Christ and what it will become when he returns in glory, one, holy, catholic, and apostolic.

With this aim in mind, Calvin frequently said that it was useless for the preacher merely to declare the truths of the Bible and leave the congregation to accept them or not without more ado. "'It is not enough," says [St Paul], "to preach what is good and useful. For if men were well-disposed and received what God set before them, and were so teachable that they could put their minds and hearts into line with it, to subject themselves to what is good, it would be enough to have

The Stimuli of Exhortations

said, "This is what God declares to us". But since men are malicious, are ungrateful, are perverse, ask only for lies in place of the truth, readily go astray, and after they have known God turn again and distance themselves from him — for this reason it is necessary," says St Paul, "for us to be held as it were forcibly, and for God, having faithfully taught us, to exhort us to persist in obedience to his Word" . . . And moreover, let us bear being admonished when [the preacher] has declared to us what is good and exhorts us to keep to it. And again, when we have been warned, if we are reproved, even forcibly, and [the preacher] uses reproofs which are harsh to us, let us know that it is for our profit' (CO 53.332$^{14\text{-}44}$).

Therefore the people had to be urged to accept what was said. They had to be spoken to bluntly and forcefully. They had to be told when they were going wrong, or not being ready to go right. The prince's ambassador, he says, will not speak harshly as a private person; but when he has to deliver his message, 'he speaks in a way that shows he is not pretending . . . Now, when God sends us and puts his Word in our mouths, have we to go [into the pulpit] with such silly simpleness that it makes men despise God and mock the Word which we carry? Not at all; not at all' (CO 53.21^{55}-22^{8}). And a little later in the same sermon: 'Moreover, let us learn that God does not intend there to be churches as places for people to make merry and laugh in, as if a comedy were being acted here. But there must be majesty in his Word, by which we may be moved and affected' (CO 53.24^{48}).

It is noticeable that Calvin's treatment of his congregation is not uniform over the years. And there is a very good reason for this. The series that we have chosen to examine more closely were all, with the exception of *Isaiah*, preached during the period of particular difficulty in Geneva. The opposition to Calvin's reforms had been building up until it came to a head in 1553. We, with the advantage of knowing what was going to happen in the next year or two, can see that the opposition was defeated in that year, when once the decisive point at issue (where the right to excommunicate lay) was decided according to Calvin's interpretation. But things seemed very different at the time. Two days after he had begun the sermons on 1

Timothy he was writing to Bullinger that matters were still in suspense in Geneva (CO 15.233[5-6]). Six weeks later, to Farel, 'Our enemies are plotting — what, I do not know' (CO 15.298[24-26]). The day after Christmas Day there is a cry of despair to Wolf, that his only comfort is that he will soon be dead (CO 15.357[37-38]). Even after the City elections of February 1555 had turned out satisfactorily for him he could still tell Bullinger that he expected to be banished.

As if all this were not enough, there was also the long-standing trouble between Geneva and her more powerful neighbour and former ally, Bern. Geneva wanted a treaty of alliance to be ratified; Bern was unwilling. It required years of patient negotiations, in which Calvin was involved (he had to interrupt his sermons on 1 Timothy and Deuteronomy for visits to Bern), before the affair was settled in 1557. The quarrel was exacerbated in the earlier years by the intense antagonism of some of the Bern ministers against Calvin and his theology.

This brief résumé may serve as an explanation of the heightened tone in the sermons of these years. It is clear that Calvin was living under great stress, and it is not surprising that the stress shows itself in the sermons. Those preached later, in the years of comparative peacefulness, are in an altogether quieter tone. Yet even in the stormy years the outbursts are not very frequent. For he was not preaching only to the members of the opposition, who would form but a small part of the congregation. The most of the hearers would have been either sympathisers or at least the uncommitted, who are always in the majority.

There was, however, always one man in the congregation at whom he directed his sermons. And that was himself: 'Seeing that the assembled flock ought to hear the Word of God by the mouth of a man, he that speaks must certainly testify that it is all in good faith, and that he has such a reverence for the teaching he proclaims that he means to be the first to be obedient to it [*s'y ranger*], and that he wishes to declare that he is not only imposing a law on others but that the subjection is in common and that it is for him to make a start' (CO 53.257[41]-258[10]). An indication of his own involvement appears in the almost universal use of 'we' and 'us' and the rare address of 'you'. The message and its application are directed at preacher and congregation alike.

The purpose of 'teaching, reproof, correction, and training in righteousness' is 'that the man of God may be complete [Calvin's word is *entier*], and that he may be formed to every good work'. But completeness does not come in a day. The Christian life is a journey, a course from Baptism to death, a progressive sanctification, a continual putting to death of sin and a continual striving after obedience, a daily putting off of the old man and a daily putting on of Christ. But Calvin does not so preach the slowness and gradualness of sanctification as to weaken the urgency of each sermon, as if repentance could safely be deferred until tomorrow, obedience to a more fitting season. On the contrary, precisely because growth in grace is slow, the opportunities are not to be wasted.

The text will determine the precise direction of the exhortation. In 1 Timothy the object will now be the ministers (e.g. 'This is a true saying, "If any man desire the office of a bishop, he desires a good work"' 1 Tim. 3.1-7, furnishing texts for Sermons XX-XXIV), now the deacons (e.g. 'Likewise must the deacons be grave . . .' 1 Tim. 3.8-13 — Sermon XXV), now servants (e.g. 'Let as many servants as are under the yoke . . .' 1 Tim. 6.1-2 — Sermon XLVI), now women (e.g. 'In like manner also that women . . .' 1 Tim. 2.9-15 — Sermons XVII-XIX). Besides these clear indications, however, others will be slipped in as the preacher thinks needful. Thus in Sermon XVIII the verse 'I suffer not a woman . . . to usurp authority over the man' (1 Tim. 2.12) leads Calvin on not only to ministers (which is in accord with the context) but then to a broader application to magistrates — that is, City Councillors (CO 53.218[52]ff.).

The sermons are saved from fragmentation into addresses to particular groups, and the unity of the congregation is preserved, by continual generalisation. In Sermon XVIII on the text about women he will say: '*Voilà*, then, a general teaching that we have to gather from the passage . . .' (CO 53.211[48-49]). Or again: 'So much, then, for this word that St Paul uses when he says, "If someone desires the office of a bishop". Now, this is to be extended even further; for we have to gather a general message [*doctrine*]. It is, that in whatever state we may be . . .' (CO 53.238[43-48]). Those who do not belong to a group that is being addressed have little time for relaxing into pharisaical self-congratulation before they find themselves being drawn into the exhortation.

Much of the exhortation concerns general graces and sins and is expressed in a way that could be relevant to any century. So on Job 23.12, 'I have not rejected the commandment of his lips; I have locked it up (*je l'ay serré*)'. This, he says, is like laying up a treasure, but not for our own use exclusively: 'When we have this treasure of the message of salvation hidden in our consciousness, it is not only for our own use, our own profit, but also to edify our neighbours' (Sermon XC. CO 34.357[23-27]). Or on Deut. 4.32: 'And as I have said that this teaching is very useful, so much the more ought we to be heedful to observe it. For by nature we are inclined to go astray. For even if we have no opportunities [*occasions*] before our eyes, yet each one of us deceives and deludes himself. And then, the devil does not cease to present us with many illusions, to obscure our thinking and to make us decline from the true and pure religion. Seeing, then, there is such a vice within us, seeing we are surrounded by so many dangers, let us learn to make our profit from this teaching' (Sermon XXVII. CO 26.201[56]-202[11]). Or on 1 Tim. 6.12, 'Fight the good fight of faith . . .': 'So then, when these temptations come before us and we are stirred up to fight, let us make this teaching of St Paul's our defence. It is that faith is never without combats; that we cannot serve God without being men of war. And why? Because we have enemies before us; we are surrounded on all sides. And so there is need for us to be accustomed to fight battles or we shall fail. Since, then, none can serve God without being exercised in endurance and [being] in the midst of those afflictions by which God's children are tormented, let us see to it that we do not renounce our faith; but we must still march on' (Sermon L. CO 53.596[6-19]).

This is the usual tone and these are the usual sort of subjects that are treated in the sermons. They are things that have been said in every century; the quiet, persistent call to frame our lives according to the teaching of Holy Scripture. The reader will have noted the low key in which he speaks. There is no threshing himself into a fever of impatience or frustration, no holier-than-thou rebuking of the people, no begging them in terms of hyperbole to give some physical sign that the message has been accepted. It is simply one man, conscious of his sins, aware how little progress he makes and how hard it is to be a doer of the Word, sympathetically passing on to his people (whom he knows to have the same sort of problems as himself) what God has said to them and to him. We even notice that in the examples given above there is not one direct imperative in the second person. He is content to pass on the message, to declare how unwilling 'we' are to accept it and how weak 'we' are in general, how slack and rebellious, and then to use the firm but gentle first person plural imperative, 'let us . . .'

Yet he is never weak. Sin is never condoned, never treated lightly. Its gravity in the sight of God, the eternal curse that lies upon every departure from the Law, every falling short of God's standard, are continually and relentlessly driven home. But because he is always aware of his solidarity in sin with all his hearers, there is no moral brutality of the strong Christian bullying the weak.

Nevertheless, we must certainly not give the impression that butter would not melt in his mouth. There are some things that rouse his anger. One is injustice, and especially injustice under the cloak of legality. Another is deliberate and flagrant opposition to the Gospel by those who had sworn to uphold it. The Romanists receive gentler treatment than the opponents on the Genevan Councils in the bad years. And he can get very angry indeed in the sermons of 1554-1555. By nature he was, as Colladon put it, 'inclined *à colere*' (CO 21.117[36-37]); which we may take to mean short-tempered and irritable. The fault was made worse, Colladon adds, 'in that his marvellously quick intelligence, the lack of comprehension (*l'indiscretion*) of many, the infinite multitude and variety of business on behalf of God's Church, and towards the end of his life his serious chronic illnesses, made him *chagrin* (peevish) *et difficile*' (CO 21.117[37-41]).

Calvin himself was aware of his fault and regretted it. But he made no apology for anger on behalf of the Gospel and justice

— as in Sermon CXIX on Job, probably preached in December 1554: 'Well now, then, what have we to note from this passage? In the first place it is that we ought not to condemn all anger. When we see a man get heated and angry, we must not always ascribe it to vice — as we see those mockers of God who will say, "Ho! need he storm like that? Need he get angry? Doesn't he know how to use a peaceful manner?" They will blaspheme God wickedly; they will spite him — as we see many who want to overthrow all good doctrine and ask for nothing but corruptions everywhere... Now, having done that, they would like us to dissimulate or even approve of all that they have done, and then in the pulpit just tell a few stories, so that there may be no reproofs. "That's the way to go on," they will say, 'Don't they know how to preach without getting angry?" *Et comment*? Is it possible for us to see a mortal, frail creature raise himself like that against the majesty of God, treading all good doctrine under foot, and yet bear it patiently?' (CO 35.11^{55}-12^{22}).

For an example we may take an indictment of some of the Genevan judges. The date is the morning of September 23, 1554. The text is 1 Tim. 1.5; 'Now the end of the commandment is love... out of a good conscience'. '*Voilà* what "a good conscience" means. For let one hide the fact as much as he likes, we have to go a long way, we have to go post-haste, if we are to discover it. It is not to be found here. It is a very rare plant. And since this is so, we see what "good" consciences men have in really solemn matters, of which the consequences are grave. When they come to it they have hardly a scruple of making a complete mock of God in solemn oaths. I am not talking now of the oaths they utter in the shops and round the markets, where God's name will be most horribly cut to pieces (and just as they make empty oaths, they also do everything with perjury — they do not know how to sell anything for a *sou* without being either a liar or a perjurer)... I am not speaking, as I say, of oaths of that sort. But even in the law courts everything is corrupted — where oaths are ordained in order that God's name may be taken with the reverence and majesty due to it. A man will come there. He is made to raise his hand to heaven. It is as if he were there actually before the majesty of God to which he appeals as witness of what he wants to say.

Alas! he will not cease to perjure himself openly . . . And nevertheless those who are present know very well that the judges themselves were witnesses of the event, that they were present when it happened; and at the end of a couple of days they will be called, and they will have no shame in swearing that they know nothing about it . . . And who are they? [Did Calvin pause at this point, to make the culprits think they were going to be named from the pulpit?] There are not just three or four. It is everyone that thinks he can get away with it . . . And do we think that such impiety, so enormous and by which God is provoked to such anger, remains unpunished? We know what a curse he pronounces on those that take his name in vain. Those that make such a mock of God, that blaspheme him horribly, these are the "good witnesses" of this place. The honour of this city must be torn in pieces [reading *dechiré* for *dechiffré* (deciphered), which does not make sense] when things are so dissolute and confused. In short, when a traveller has stopped here only three days, he will certainly have seen that there is no longer any honesty or modesty before men; and the report of our infamy will fly a hundred leagues hence' (Sermon III. CO 53.38^{1}-39^{8}).

We may now see how the internal struggle in Geneva is reflected in the sermons.

Things are in a fearful state, he says in Sermon V on 1 Timothy. No-one worries about the blasphemies uttered, the dishonouring of God, the denial of truth. There is more uprightness even among the Turks. 'If a man dares to open his mouth to reprove the vices and licentiousness or the singing of shameful and filthy songs — if anyone wants to speak one word about it, they will make out that he has spoken against the honour of Geneva. So that it is not possible nowadays to rebuke vices without being accused of having committed a great crime. And look at this city of marvellous sanctity! You think it is extremely holy! It would be better for all the world to be overwhelmed than to speak of the impieties committed here — and one dare not say a word' (CO 53.57$^{38-39}$).

Geneva, he says on December 26, is a free city, a city that threw off the bonds of Rome. 'Where, then, is the liberty today? Not in faith, but in every kind of evil among those that are entirely hardened, that have no shame. And when they see that they are allowed to do whatever they like, they think that everything is lawful for them. For them there is neither law nor reason, no honest living, no shame' (CO 53.305[18-26]). The very Papists are better than the Genevese. 'As for me, I can say that I am ashamed to preach the Word of God in this place when there are such villainies as we see. If it were left to my own wishes, I would desire God to take me out of the world, that I might not have to live for three days in the disorder that is here' (CO 53.316[23-32]). And on January 20: 'Would to God that such men had got back the pastors that they like — and that it had been for their salvation! I would wish to be far enough away from Geneva. And would to God I had never come within a hundred leagues of the place to do their pleasure! so long as there had been men who desired their salvation. But what? They want to have devils!' (CO 53.438[15-22]).

The elections to the City Councils were due to be held through the first week in February, 1555. Calvin anticipated them with his usual nervous anxiety. On the morning of Sunday, January 27, towards the end of his sermon (1 Tim. 5.1. 'Rebuke not an elder, but entreat him as a father') he took occasion to warn the congregation about responsible voting. 'We have need today of this admonition; for the election approaches of those that are to be established in the government of this Republic. Now, I ask you, how are they behaving in the election? For I need not wait till next Sunday to say something which is only too plain. When it is a question of electing and choosing the magistrates [i.e. councillors], they ought to be here to call on the name of God, that he would preside at the Council and that he would give them a spirit of prudence and right. But where will they be? In the taverns, or at play. And those who have a vote are the least frequenters of sermons. It is true that one will hardly see them coming any more to church on other days. Nevertheless, they will be the first to present themselves at the General Council and want to have the strongest voice.... Yet it is there that they will throw off all restraint, and there will be even greater disorder. On such a day one will see them come with a rascally impudence — and they will be in groups, as if they wanted to make their presence felt. And where have they come from? From an alehouse — instead of wanting to be here to call upon the name of God and to look into themselves, "Now, come! We have today to elect men who will rule in God's name. But there is no question of choosing them at our whim, for they are to preside here in the authority of God" . . .' (CO 53.452$^{3\text{-}32}$).

The following Sunday saw the start of the elections. The text, 1 Tim. 5.7-12, supplied in its last verse a reference to choosing or electing': 'Let not a widow be elected until she is at least sixty years old'. Calvin takes up the word and applies it to the subject on all their minds: 'For when elections are due to be held (as today the governors have to be elected, and tomorrow, and tomorrow; and all this week it is necessary to provide for the state of the City and the order of justice, which is a very holy thing), how many are there who think of God? The most solemn election is to be held now. Those who will come to it, where are some of them? I have just met some of these louts, that I could point the finger at — but there is no need; they are known well enough. Some were going towards the Bourg de Four [a square at the end of the Rue de l'Hotel de Ville, and hence away from St Pierre]; others were sauntering about down here — it seemed to them that they would have no leisure for breakfast unless they chose service time. I saw that with my own eyes as I came to church. And is it not a quite notorious shame? . . . so, then, let us think that it is not without cause declared to us, when men have to be elected to a public office, that we must go with reverence, with carefulness; otherwise it will provoke God's wrath if the seat of justice is polluted by men being put there who have neither zeal nor affection to honour and serve him' (CO 53.475^{45}-476^{16}).

In fact, the elections turned out highly satisfactorily for Calvin's cause (though this will have been due as much to the large numbers of French refugees being given the vote as to his exhortations). His anxiety was not at rest, however; and with good reason. The Perrinist uprising took place on Thursday, May 16. It was firmly dealt with and was all over in an evening; but if it had been prosecuted with more determination it could well have effected a seizure of power, perhaps even a massacre of the French. It is a pity, from our point of view at the moment, that this could not have taken place during one of Calvin's preaching weeks, for there must surely have been a reference to it the following morning. As it is, the first sermon after this fell on Sunday, May 19. The text he had come to was 2 Tim. 2.1-3: 'Thou therefore, my son, be strong in the grace that is in Jesus Christ . . . endure hardness as a good soldier of Jesus Christ'. There is no open mention of the riot at all. The nearest he came to it was: 'since Jesus Christ is our Captain and we are under him, let us not be afraid. Although our enemies are full of the spirit of murder, full of rage, of malice, and of treason, and do worse than it seemed possible for them, let us follow boldly. And why? We shall be secure under the hand of him who has promised and declared that nothing that has been given to him by God his Father shall perish, but that he will guard it so well and so surely that he will render a good account of it at the last day' (CO 53.100^{55}-101^{10}). But this and what follows is couched in such general terms that it could refer to any military threat to Geneva from an outside enemy. There can be little doubt that the congregation applied it for themselves to the topic that everyone was talking about.

In a year or two the tone of the sermons is quite changed. Now Calvin can look back on the troubles and call for thanksgiving to God for deliverance. Thus on Isa. 14.3-8, preached on February 26, 1557: 'our ingratitude will be the more wicked and inexcusable when we do not follow what is here remonstrated to us by the Prophet. For this poor city, has it not been even in the depths? Did it not seem that, although it was not assailed with great violence, it was going to be destroyed little by little? And how did God work? So then, if ever people had occasion to sing a hymn to God and speak of the heavenly help and of the succour that we have experienced from his hand, it is certain that we ought to have our mouths open to glorify God, seeing that he had mercy on this place' (SC II. 43$^{25\text{-}31}$).

He even had the luxury of being able to preach without the danger of provoking a major disturbance: 'And for a time we saw the same in Geneva. No sooner had one preached than they had to find fault [SC reads *complotter* for ms. *construire*. I should prefer *condemner* for the sake of the sense]. They had to run to the City Hall: "What's all this! What's going on, messieurs? Look how he is shouting out and whom he is fastening on. And what will the people down there say? It looks as if listening to him will lead to utter confusion — and it will be your fault". *Voilà* how it used to be' (SC II.631[25-29]).

In the next volume of Isaiah sermons (Isa. 30-41) the editors themselves were surprised at the paucity of references to current events, inside or outside Geneva. It was not that nothing of moment was happening at the time. On the contrary, the dispute between Geneva and Bern was still unresolved. Geneva for some time expected an attack by Savoy. In Paris the Evangelicals were being subjected to severe persecution; one of the two representatives sent from Geneva to help them was killed in September 1557. And yet of all this there is no explicit word in the sermons. It is possible to read between the lines and take this or that apparently general statement as a specific reference that the congregation would have understood; but there is nothing certain. Even when the inhabitants had been instructed to go to church on October 13, 1557 in view of the threat of a siege by Savoy there is nothing, although Calvin had reached a passage suitable for such an application. Isa. 37.1-4 is part of the story of the siege of Jerusalem by Nebuchadnezzar. There is just a very general reference to the wars in other parts of Europe: 'Now, when we see [God's] punishing blows and even hear the thud of them although we do not feel them, is it not time, if ever it was, to return to God and humble ourselves? . . . Look at the wars that we see before our eyes. The very sounds reverberate in the air. And yet, when one says, "Such and such a country is entirely despoiled. Look at what a change and revolution there has been!" — although one speaks like that, oh well! all that is just news. It all passes and we do not think of it' (SC III. ms. fr. 18.fol.268ᵛ. See also the Introduction).

The only current affair that receives direct mention in this set is the renewed threat from the Turks and in particular the alliance between them and European powers. The Turks appear in no fewer than four sermons. Now France is like Judah, who 'went down into Egypt and fortified itself in the strength of Pharaoh' (Isa. 30.2). France not only allies herself with the Turks and fights alongside them, but even adopts their customs and their dress (ms. fr. fol. 2ʳ). Later, the account of Hezekiah showing the Babylonian envoys his treasures furnishes Calvin with the opportunity to censure both the Emperor and the French King: 'We have to note that at that time the King of Babylon in relation to the King of Assyria was like the Sophy [i.e. Persia] and the Turk today. While the one was hindered, the other carried on with his activities. And this is how, on one side or the other, they drew kings into alliances ... We still see these practices carried on today. While one woos the Turk, the other is after the Sophy of Persia' (SC III. ms. fr. 18. fol.410ᵛ).

All through the years we come upon fairly frequent anti-Romanist polemic. This is more often directed against practice than against points of doctrine — the invocation of saints, pilgrimages, compulsory observance of fast-days, non-preaching bishops and the like. Any explanation of doctrine is undertaken in broad terms without technical detail. 'In the Papacy, I ask you, what are the articles that are held as most certain? If someone denied the resurrection of the dead or eternal life, it would not be so great a heresy as to deny purgatory. And what certainty have they of purgatory? What Angel — or what devil — revealed to them that purgatory exists? They have built it in their own heads. And although they have tried to get testimonies from Holy Scripture, in the end they are left abashed, so that they have no other defence for their purgatory than antiquity. "Ho *voilà!* one has always held it like that". *Voilà donc* the foundation of faith according to the Papist doctors' (CO 53.45[23-36]).

Occasionally it is the schoolmen that are the target; but still in general terms and without getting led into the quick-sands of medieval theological conjecture. The expression 'profane fables' in 1 Tim. 4.7 gives rise to these comments: 'Now, such errors [as I have just mentioned] should be detestable to us. But there is an evil which is more hidden, and which is unknown to ordinary people. For even if the doctrine of the Papists were not false (as it is), even if it were not perverse, it would still be profane ... Why? They have questions that they discuss about things in which there is no profit. When a man has known all the questions debated in the Papist schools of theology, there is nothing but wind. They torment themselves more and more and never come to a conclusion. For they put forward questions that can only be resolved by guess-work. And when a man wants to search out secrets of God of which there is no declaration in Holy Scripture, is he not falling into an abyss?' (CO 53.378[37-54]).

If the anti-Romanist polemic is found tiresome by many modern readers, they should remind themselves of the situation in which the sermons were preached. Geneva had accepted the Reform only in 1536. Not until about 1550 would there emerge a generation that had not been brought up in a Roman Catholic city, with its own bishop and its general religious life. For them the various churches would be associated with celebrations of the Mass. They would be used to images and the current liturgical practices. The exodus of priest, monks, and nuns in 1535-1536 certainly did not mean that there were no Romanists left in Geneva. The *Registres* show how some of the old habits and practices lingered on in a usually quiet sort of way. Calvin had to win people over to become Bible Christians, and the negative side of that was to convince them that the Romanist claim to possess the truth was contradicted by the Bible itself. Nevertheless, it is noticeable that this polemic, harsh and sarcastic as it often was, lacked the fierce anger bestowed on lawlessness and licentiousness in the city.

That we have concentrated in the latter part of this chapter on the exceptional passages in the sermons will leave the wrong impression unless we quickly redress the balance. Even in the years of crisis the examples we have given are only passages within sermons whose general tenor is very different. We remember that Calvin was expounding Holy Scripture in a way that he thought would be profitable for his people and build them up as children of God. His talk, therefore, is of God's revealing himself as our Father, of what God has done for us in Jesus Christ, of his care for his people and of our trust and obedience and perseverance. The stimuli of exhortations have for their aim the building up of the believer in the head and heart knowledge of God in Christ.

Therefore we will end the chapter with a piece of exhortation on a page opened at random in *Job*. It is Sermon CXXX (Job 34.10-15). 'Moreover, if we want to understand this teaching [that God is righteous] and to be convinced of it, it is necessary in the first place that each of us shall scrutinise himself and think carefully what he is. For what is the reason why we are so resentful and God cannot content us, whatever he may do, and we always have the audacity of rising up against him, except that we are blinded by vain flatteries and that each one thinks he is righteous and does not consider his sins? And so, when we shall have this judgment in us of recognising our faults, it is certain that all answering back at God will cease and be resolved, and in humility each will come to say, "Lord, thou hast treated me in such a way that I cannot help knowing thy righteousness; and I glorify thee." *Mais quoy*? We cannot hold back from deceiving ourselves; and although we know that we have no reply, we always want to lessen our vices, yes, and cover them up, although they are worse than notorious. Now, are we so put to sleep in our faults by our hypocrisy? Then it is easy for us to rise up against God. And so it is the true remedy when men would recognise that God is righteous, to ascribe to him the praise that is his due, that in the first place they call themselves to account, and accuse themselves, and condemn themselves. Then it will cost them nothing to acknowledge that God is righteous' (CO 35.144[48]-145[26]).

Part Five
Form and Style

Chapter 12

The Pattern of the Sermons

There has come down to us (so far as I know) no contemporary description of Calvin while preaching, his demeanour, his expressions and gestures, his tones of voice. All that we have is the written or printed word, with the sentences arranged according to the conventions of sixteenth century punctuation. The editors of *Supplementa Calviniana* have sought to help their readers to an appreciation of the original spoken words by a more sophisticated and flexible punctuation. To this, however, we need to add our own imagination and commonsense. If in the end we have to admit that much is lost, yet we have the solace of knowing that in one way we have an advantage over the hearers of the sermons in that we can take our time over them, reading a sentence or passage twice, pausing for consideration, and so on, whereas they were carried forward at the preacher's pace.

For the literary critic it is no bad thing to be deprived of gesture and changes of voice. Driven back to the printed word, he must ask whether the preacher is able, without those aids and thus relying only on the use of words in sentences, to convey his meaning intelligibly, forcefully, and persuasively. For clarity, force, and persuasiveness are the three necessary ingredients in preaching like Calvin's.

It would be possible to treat of his style according to the injunctions of the rhetoricians. Calvin knew his Quintilian and his Cicero and no doubt also his contemporary Rudolf Agricola. But like Bullinger and Melanchthon and Bucer, he used rhetoric rather as a tool in the interpretation of documents than for a conscious directive in his own writing. Moreover, as Bullinger said in reply to the Romanist charge that the Reformers were at fault to use rhetoric to interpret St Paul, the rules of rhetoric are only an analysis in technical terms of everyday speech. To apply the language of the rhetoricians to these sermons would be possible; but it would convey a false impression. The object of the classical writers on rhetoric was to train young men as public speakers, especially as pleaders in courts of law. The framework of such speeches consisted in the successive steps in the case that was being pleaded.

Calvin, however, followed a different path by confining himself to the continuous exposition of his documents. In terms of sixteenth century law studies he was, both in his lectures and in his preaching, rather on the side of the 'old' method, with its continuous exposition, than of the 'modern'. One of his regular hearers, indeed, wrote that he lectured more in the scholastic than in the rhetorical style, 'much like that which was used in lectures in former days' (CO 42.4).

It would also be possible to analyse these sermons in terms of a movement of statement of text, exegesis, interpretation, exposition, application, exhortation, and any other of the abstract nouns ending in -ion that were so dear to writers on the art of preaching like Andreas Hyperius. But what would be left at the end would not look much like one of Calvin's sermons.

The form of this preaching is determined by the movement of the text. The preacher does not so much move forward from point to point as be borne onwards by the movement of his author's thought. Even so, this is not a simple, uncomplicated stepping from clause to clause; for within each clause there is movement and counter-movement of one sort or another. The sermons are like rivers, moving strongly in one direction, alive with eddies and cross-currents, now thundering in cataracts, now a calm mirror of the banks and the sky; but never still, never stagnant.

Calvin's intention (like that of the medieval theology lecturers) was to expound each passage. Usually this entailed the continuous exposition of sentence by sentence, sometimes of clause by clause. After a brief preface to remind the congregation of what the previous passage had said, and thus to set the present verses within their context, he would embark on the exposition of the sentences, usually rendering them in a slightly different (sometimes very different) form from the head text; this partly because he was translating direct as he went along, partly for the sake of clarification by paraphrasing. The exposition will consist where necessary of simple exegesis and the unravelling of any difficulties (perhaps discrepancies with other passages of Scripture, which, again like medieval lecturing, had always to be reconciled); after this he will apply the place to 'our' use so that 'we' may profit from it and be 'edified'.

A sermon that follows this pattern closely is number LXXX on Job (CO 34.227-240). The text is chapter 21. 13-15: 'They pass their days in good, and in a moment they descend to the sepulchre. Yet they say to God, 'Depart from us, for we do not wish to know thy ways. What is the Almighty, that we should serve him? or what profit will there be to pray to him?"'.

1. He reminds the congregation of what he said yesterday.
2. Verse 13. 'God will permit the despisers of his majesty *to go to the sepulchre in a minute of time*, after they have had a good time all their life'.

Ps. 73.4ff. (of which a brief exposition) may be compared with this passage.

There is a contrast between the often easy deaths of the ungodly and the death-pangs of believers.

But God defers his judgments to the next world; and therefore we must raise our minds above this fleeting world, when God will judge the ungodly.

Therefore, let us not be like those who despise God and have all their happiness in this world. But rather let us prefer to be wretched here and look to God to give us his bounty hereafter.

'See what believers are admonished of here'.

3. Verse 14. 'Now Job consequently declares how the wicked reject God entirely. *They say to him, "Depart from us, for we do not wish to know thy ways".*'

The wicked wish to be free from God. We see them trying to get away from him by claiming they can do as they like.

'*We do not wish for thy ways.*' To be near God or far from him does not refer to his essence and majesty. It is to be obedient or disobedient to his Word.

'Now *voici* a passage from which we can gather good and useful teaching':
   (1) The root and foundation of a good life is to have God always before us.
      (a) How can a man leave the corruption of his nature?
      (b) He must be reformed by God, for he cannot reform himself.
      (c) We are so blind that we do not know the right way. We think evil is good until God enlightens us.

'So then, do we wish to walk as we should? Let us make a start at this point — that is, of drawing near to our God. How do we draw near? First of all, let us know that nothing is hidden from him; everyone must come to a reckoning before him, and he must be the Judge, even of our thoughts' (CO 34.232[7-13]).

Voilà, so much for the first'.
   (2) God will judge us by his Word, the two-edged sword.
      (a) Therefore we must draw near to him.
      (b) And this means, to him in his Word, in which he comes to us.
      (c) Therefore our greatest misery is to be without God's Word; our greatest blessing is when he gives it to us.
      (d) Those who will not submit to his Word show that they are God's enemies.
      (e) Let us always be willing and obedient.

'*Voilà* what we have to note from this passage — that we may not only have God before our eyes, but also love him to care for us and lead us' (CO 34.234[8-11]).

4. Verse 15. 'Now, after Job has shown here such blasphemy on the part of the wicked and the despisers of God, he adds that they say, "*What is the Almighty that we should serve him and what profit will it bring us to pray to him?*"
   (1) The pride of the ungodly.
      (a) Pride is the principal vice of the wicked, as humility is the sovereign virtue in believers — the mother of all virtue.
      (b) Their pride is trust in their own wisdom.
      (c) Swollen with presumption, they do just what they like.

The Pattern of the Sermons

(2) *'Who is the Almighty, that we should serve him?'*

(a) They do not use these words, but this is in their mind; and sometimes God makes them betray themselves.

(b) They acknowledge God's existence, but not his authority.

(c) But believers must submit themselves to God as those that are his children, created in his image, redeemed by the death and passion of his only Son, and called to be his household, as children and heirs.

'When, then, we have made all these comparisons — I pray you, if we have hearts of iron or steel, ought they not to be softened? If we are swollen with arrogance and bursting with it, must not all that poison be purged, that so we may come with true humility to obey God?' (CO 34.236$^{33\text{-}40}$).

(d) He refers to the preface to the Ten Commandments: 'I am the Eternal, thy God'.

(i) 'The Eternal' — that is, the Creator.

(ii) 'thy God' — the Father of his people.

(iii) 'that brought thee out of the land of Egypt, out of the house of bondage' — that is, redeemed us from the depths of hell by our Lord Jesus Christ.

(iv) Therefore we must dedicate ourselves entirely to the service of God.

(v) God adds promises to his service, that he will be our Father, the protector of our life, that he will pardon our sins, and will accept our feeble service without examining it rigorously and hypercritically.

(3) *'What is the profit of serving God?'*

(a) If we flee from God, we become servants to our own desires or to the devil.

(b) Freedom from God's service is bondage.

(c) The service of God is more honourable than possessing a kingdom.

(4) 'Moreover, let us extend this even further, as Job has done'.

(a) The wicked think they can live well or ill as they like, because God's punishments are not apparent.

(b) But we must hold to the truth of what Isaiah said: 'There is good fruit for the righteous' (3.10). When we see confusion in the world and it seems a mockery to serve God, we must trust in him that he will not disappoint our hope.
(c) God himself is our reward, as it says in Ps. 16.5 and Gen. 15.1.
5. 'Now, there is still one word to note. It is that after Job had spoken of the service of God, in the second place he put prayer.'
(1) Although service to our fellows is service to God, more is required — 'prayers and orisons'.
(2) A life unstained by gross vices and yet without religion or faith is not acceptable to God.
(3) The principal service of God is to call upon him.
(4) The conclusion: A life approved and accepted by God is one that trusts in him and has recourse to him and is loving towards our neighbours. 'When, then, our life is thus ruled, it is the true service of God.'
Bidding to prayer, relevant to the substance of the sermon.

We are not at the moment concerned with the teaching of the sermon (although no doubt the reader will have perceived very many of the points made in earlier chapters), but only with the form. We see how Calvin could keep to the pattern and movement of the text and yet allow himself at each stage room to look at the verses or clauses in the broad context of the Biblical message. Above all, he is not enslaved by his method, but uses it as far as it suits his purpose. The three verses of the text receive very unequal treatment, with verse 15 being given the chief place. With an hour at his disposal he can develope his arguments steadily.

We note also how the several members are begun and concluded by certain regular formulae. These are very common indeed in all the sermons. 'St Paul goes on to say . . .' 'Moses now adds . . .' And this will be followed by a new rendering or a paraphrase of the text. And to end a section there will be 'So now we see the Prophet's meaning.'; *'Voilà pour un item*' ('So much for one point'); *'Voilà* in sum what we

The Pattern of the Sermons

have to note in this passage'; and many more. Such formulae are a sort of spoken punctuation, marking the beginning and ending of periods.

Not all the sermons follow their text so neatly and easily as the one we have just summarised. Sometimes Calvin will concentrate on a single verse and neglect the rest. For example, one would have thought that 1 Tim. 3.16 would provide a sermon that followed its movement closely, giving us sections in the following order:

1. 'Without controversy great is the mystery of godliness';
2. 'God was manifested in the flesh';
3. 'justified in the Spirit';
4. 'seen of Angels';
5. 'was preached unto the Gentiles';
6. 'believed on in the world';
7. 'received up into glory'.

We might not expect him to go so far as the divisions and subdivisions of Lancelot Andrewes' sermon on this text (*Ninety-six Sermons* 1. 32ff.), but what we get is surprising. The sermon (*1 Timothy XXVII.* CO 53.317-330) is plainly Calvinian in substance and language, but it is far from conforming to the usual pattern. After a short introduction referring back to 'this morning', and so placing the verse in its context, that the Gospel is a treasure committed to the Church (3.15), he summarises his text at some length (CO 53.317^{40}-318^{28}). As he does so, we notice that he is concentrating on two parts of the text, 'mystery' and 'God was manifested in the flesh' (for he accepted the Stephanus 1550 reading θεος although he knew the alternative ὅς and ascribed it to the Vulgate and Erasmus). It is 'God was manifested in the flesh' that was to provide the real text of the sermon; that is, the mystery of the fact that God was manifested in the flesh. He therefore explains the meaning of the word 'flesh' in this context, and then of '*God* was manifested', and afterwards of 'God *was manifested*'. All this occupies more than eight of the eleven and a half columns in CO. The clause 'justified in the Spirit' is treated towards the end in rather more than one column. He concludes by returning to the word 'mystery' or 'secret'. The main body of the sermon is thus less than an exposition of the text than teaching on its general meaning — how the union of the Godhead and manhood in Jesus Christ is to be understood, and what it means for 'us' that God was manifested in the flesh.

When we speak, therefore, of a typical pattern of Calvin's sermons, it must be remembered that he employed the expository method he had adopted quite freely and departed from it when he conceived occasion demanded. In this, we may note, the sermons differ a little from the lectures, where normally each verse receives due treatment.

Chapter 13

The Familiar Style

The word that Calvin used to describe what he regarded as the most suitable style for the preacher is '*familière*'. Its meaning and implications will be understood from the following quotation: 'Moreover, when St Paul says here, *teach otherwise* [1 Tim. 1.3], it refers not only to the substance but also to the form, as they call it, and to the style. This will be a little obscure unless it is explained more fully. There are two things in teaching. There is the subject of which one speaks, or the matter.' He takes as example that God is our Father in Jesus Christ. 'Then, after that there is the manner of drawing out the consequences (*deduire les choses*) . . . It is necessary for [the substance] to be shown in a style proper to teaching'. And he shows how the original subject, God is our Father in Jesus Christ, may be explained more fully and applied. 'So, when these consequences have been drawn out, and when always we try to make Scripture *familière*, so that we know that it is God who is speaking to us, *voilà* the two things comprised in teaching' (CO 53. 18[41]-19[18]).

'We always try to make Scripture *familière*'. He plainly meant more than that he wanted the people to become familiar with the Bible in the sense of 'knowing their Bibles'. *Familière* might be better rendered by the word 'personal', used in the colloquial modern sense — to make the message of Scripture a personal matter, not just a collection of historical ideas; 'so that we know that it is *God* who is speaking to *us*'. Nevertheless, he is certainly thinking of *familière* in terms of language; for a little later he censures ambitious preachers who 'babble in refined language' (CO 53.19[33-34]). To make the Scriptural message *familière* Calvin used a familiar, homely style of speaking.

The familiarity of speech is made possible and also heightened by his preaching extemporarily. For he had no time to polish each sentence and paragraph as he liked to do when he had a pen in his hand. He had to use a set pattern of sentences dictated by the movement of his thought and to make do with clichés and colloquialisms. If we find the verbal repetition wearisome, we must recollect that it will have made for easier listening by those who were not too fussy about style.

Everywhere we trip over the little French word *or*. It has little real significance but is about equivalent to the English 'well' (also practically meaningless — 'Well, I don't know'), or 'now' used as an interjection. Equally ubiquitous is *donc*, a weak 'then' or 'therefore': '*Voilà donc* why Moses . . .'; 'It is, *donc*, as if God said . . .' Other maids of all work are *au reste* ('moreover'), *de faict* ('in fact'), *voilà* and *voici*, *d'autant que* ('seeing that' or 'since'), *puis* or *Et puis* ('and then'), *voire* ('indeed' — introducing a dependent clause: 'He says that almost in passing, *voire* having regard to . . .').

Every one of these examples occurs in a place opened at random in *Deuteronomy* (CO 26. columns 163-166). Indeed, as I cast my eye over these upwards of two thousand words I see examples of most of the points of Calvin's style, and there is no reason why we should not let the passage serve as the basis for nearly all that needs to be said in this connection.

The vocabulary is nearly always familiar and easy. The first sentence after the text in our random columns runs: 'Although Moses has declared that the use of the sun and of the stars is common to all nations, yet he shows that it is dedicated especially to the people whom God has chosen' (CO 26. 163[4-7]. The only word that strikes us as unusual is 'dedicated' instead of, say, 'granted'; presumably it is used to bring out the sacredness of the gift.

Only very occasionally do we find him at a loss for a word and forced to use something out of the way and then explain it. We saw an example of this in our chapter 2 with the word *redargution* (see p. 13), to the explanation of which he devotes almost half a column in CO. Another example we have met is when he ironically called Geneva 'extremely holy'. The adjec-

The Familiar Style

tive he uses here is *mout* or *moult* (from Latin *multum*), which was archaic even in the sixteenth century — Littré gives no quotation after the fifteenth century. But we must remember that some words continue in common use after they have ceased their literary life.

He is so intent on making himself understood that now and then he will think it necessary to explain a simple word which is nevertheless ambiguous from similarity of sound with a quite different word. A nice example is pointed out by Mr M. D. Miles in his Dissertation, *Calvin's New Testament Sermons*, 82. The text is Matt. 3.12, 'whose fan [RSV 'winnowing fork'] is in his hand'. Calvin realises that the word he is using, *van*, sounds little different from *vent* ('wind'). Cassell's French dictionary (1973) gives them the same sound, but there may have been a slight difference in the sixteenth century. At any rate, Calvin thought that clarification was called for: 'let us note that the Gospel is like *un van* in two ways. (I am not speaking of the *vent* which blows, but of *un van* to winnow (*vanner*) — or of a sieve (*crible*); for many will understand this word better' (CO 46.574[26-30]).

In general the vocabulary is simple. The theological language might puzzle most modern Protestant congregations in this country, but that is because they are largely ignorant of the Bible. Calvin's terminology in this respect hardly moves outside the Bible. Common words are 'justify', 'elect', 'redeem', 'sin', 'repentance', 'grace', 'prayer', 'judgment' — in fact, all the familiar language of the Old and New Testaments. Theological words from outside the Bible are only the more common ones — 'Trinity', 'sacrament' and the like. In such a Christological sermon as that on 1 Tim. 3.16 which we looked at in the last chapter there is not one of the more esoteric terms from early Trinitarian controversy. Even abstract nouns like 'incarnation' are passed over in favour of the concrete verb supplied by the text 'God was manifested in the flesh'. The term 'two natures' occurs there frequently, but it is carefully, even childishly explained: 'So then, let us note well that this word "manifested" conjoins the two natures in such a way that we have to know Jesus Christ, not at all as double, but as one only, although he has two natures. We have two eyes in our head and each eye can have its own partial sight. But when we are looking at something, if our two eyes are directed (*s'addonnent*) at what you will, our vision, which of itself is separated, is co-ordinated and united to focus (*s'addonner*) entirely on the object which is set before us. *Voici donc* such a similitude — that is, that just as we have two eyes in our head, there are in Jesus Christ two different natures' (CO 53.326[31-43]). He is drawn into the use of the word 'essence' as he refutes the teaching of the unhappy Servetus, the Anabaptist who had been executed in Geneva the previous year. Otherwise, there are no theological words at all out of the way in this sermon.

The same simplicity is seen in the sentence structure. There is a difficulty here. In the manuscripts the punctuation had to be inserted by either Raguenier or the scribe writing at his dictation. The early printed editions were punctuated presumably by the printer. For the Corpus Reformatorum edition a mixture of sixteenth and nineteenth century punctuation was used. But Calvin's punctuation in the pulpit consisted only of shorter or longer pauses and of the insertion of the formulae that we have already noticed. Thus, 'So much for one item' would normally indicate the end of a period, which would become a paragraph on the printed page. Hence we shall find that what is printed as a long sentence was often in the speaking a sequence of short sentences, each with its subject and verb, and, if a transitive verb, then also an object. One long sentence from our random columns will make this very clear.

First we give it with Corpus Reformatorum punctuation:

'As if he said, that the order of nature is certainly for everybody: we see that great and small are participants of the blessings which God does for them, the earth produces corn, wine, and all the rest, to nourish believers and unbelievers: the wicked and the despisers of God drink and eat just as we do: we see (what is more) that they abuse God's creatures with complete intemperance, and more than believers do: for he who knows that God nourishes him, will use in all sobriety and moderation, both foods, and all the rest: and he will know that he must not profane what God has dedicated to a good and moderate use: what do the wicked do?' (CO 26.163[8-21]).

Now let us read it again, with the sentences in which it was spoken:

The Familiar Style

'As if he said that the order of nature is certainly for everybody. We see that great and small are participants of the blessings which God does for them. The earth produces corn, wine, and all the rest, to nourish believers and unbelievers; the wicked and the despisers of God drink and eat just as we do. We see, what is more, that they abuse God's creatures with complete intemperance — and more than believers do. For he who knows that God nourishes him, will use in all sobriety and moderation both foods and all the rest; and he will know that he must not profane what God has dedicated to a good and moderate use. What do the wicked do?'

Instead of one long and unwieldy period, we have six terse and energetic sentences. In only three of these is there more than a single clause; and even there the first could be made into two sentences by the substitution of a full-stop for a semi-colon, if it were not that the movement is made too staccato. The third sentence consists of two sentences in the form (in French) of a main and a subsidiary clause linked by *que* (which I have rendered 'and'). In the second sentence there is a break in the thought, represented here by a dash. Perhaps Calvin's tone of voice might be brought out by an exclamation mark at this point: ' — and more than believers do!'

It is mainly by the reiterated use of *que* that he builds up sentences and heightens tension. But even so, each of the subsidiary clauses is usually a little sentence in its own right and easily referable back to the original verb. 'He says that as in passing — *voire*, having regard to the fact that he was soon to die, and that, seeing that he (*d'autant qu'il*) will not enjoy the land, he has the care of instructing the people, *in order that* they may keep themselves in covenant with God, *and that* they might be constant to it, *and that* they might not decline from it, *that* they might not change their religion, *that* they might not pervert the teaching which was given to them' (CO 26.165[50]-166[1]). Four subsidiary clauses, all depending on the original 'in order that'; but each consists of an easy subject-verb-predicate construction.

The movement of which we spoke earlier is generated not only by the movement of the text, but also by certain characteristics of style which themselves are indicative of Calvin's approach whether to theology or to any other subject. The chief ways in which this dialectic approach shows itself in his preaching style are in the frequent use of question and answer and in imaginary conversations with disputants.

There are also the numerous rhetorical questions. Several occur in our random passage. The most common is the simple *'Et pourquoy?'* ('And why [is that so]?'). 'Now, for this reason the duty of those who have to bring the Word of God is always to exhort their hearers to know and to fathom their sins. *Et pourquoy?* Not only to make them straightforwardly ashamed . . .' (CO 26.166[34-38]). *'Mais quoy?'* ('But what?') also very common, is more of an exclamation than a question. These rhetorical questions are, of course, a device to make a statement more direct and compelling. 'Now, nevertheless, God wishes the use of his creatures to be peculiar to us. And in what way? It is that we may use them as his true and legitimate heirs' (CO 26.163[23-26]).

A little later he will pile question upon question: 'For what is our state that God has left us in meanwhile? If we remain children of Adam, are we not accursed? And being rejected by God, are we not under the tyranny of Satan? Does not sin rule in us? Is this not a furnace far worse than that of Egypt?' (CO 26.164[39-45]).

The genuine question and answer, corresponding to the *quaestio* and *responsio* which is such a marked feature in the style of the lectures, occurs less often; but the example we give from Sermon CI on Job is certainly cast in the manner of the lectures. 'Here one could ask whether it is lawful for the good and believers to rejoice when they see the ruin of the wicked. But the question is almost superfluous for this passage...' (CO 34.499[50-53]). This is in the direct tradition of those medieval *summae* that were based on *questio* and *responsio*. The sentence itself drops easily into Latin: *Quaeritur an fas sit.* ...

Rather more common in the sermons is objection and reply. An imaginary opponent points out a difficulty and the preacher gives his answer of explanation. 'Now, here one could ask whether he was not concerned above all for the glory of God, which certainly ought to be preferred to the salvation of men. But the answer to that is easy...' (CO 54.129[14-17]). After the preacher's reply, the opponent counter-replies: 'But again, one could here reply that it seems to be superfluous that St Paul should endure for the elect. For cannot God save those whom he has elected and adopted before the creation of the world, without men helping him? . . . Now, it is true that God will certainly lead his own to the inheritance prepared for them; but nevertheless it is his pleasure to make men's labours effective . . .' (CO 54.129⁴⁹-130⁴). ('The reply to that is easy' is also his stock phrase in the lectures: *Responsio facilis est.*)

Dialogue, often racy, is also much in evidence. Calvin has a liking for direct speech. Instead of paraphrasing his text (as he also does frequently) with some such formula as 'it is as if he were saying . . .' he will often put it into direct speech: 'It is, then, just as if God said, "Thou didst have no hope of leaving this slavery; thou wert like a lost people; now I have drawn thee out in a miraculous way"' (CO 26.164⁵³-165¹).

But this also often appears in the form of imaginary attacks from opponents, which are usually prefixed with the angry interjection 'Ho?' 'Now, because it is difficult for men to keep calm when they hear this teaching — as we see those dogs barking against it today — these vainglorious rascals, when they want to act the learnèd doctor, they will say, "Ho! I fail to understand that." "And who are you, you miserable dog? You fail to understand it? Off to your dunghill and know what you are"' (CO 35.471²⁻⁹).

Mr Miles has shown how these conversations can be developed into a fragment of drama, with Calvin himself providing the asides for the sake of the congregation's understanding. His example is drawn from Sermon XXIV on 2 Timothy.

Calvin (aside): We see plenty of those who are most venomous when corrections and warnings are used.

Dissenters: Et quoy! Is that the way to teach? Ho! we want to be won by sweetness.

Calvin: You do? Then go and teach God his lesson.

Calvin (aside): Look at our fastidious gentlemen who cannot bear one single reproof when it is put to them! And why?

Dissenters: Ho! we want to be taught another way.

Calvin: Then go to the devil's school. He will flatter you alright — to your destruction.'

(CO 54.291[42-51]; and M. D. Miles: *Calvin's New Testament Sermons*, 103-104).'

The ready use of proverbs and similes and homely expressions gives the impression of a man of homespun speech, at ease with the common man. But, as was also the case with that countryman, Hugh Latimer, we shall be likely to find the source of the proverb or the wise saw in Erasmus' *Adagia* or Aesop's fables rather than in the daily speech of Picardy or Geneva. Some of the expressions, of course, are commonplace both then and now. 'They put the cart before the horse' — *la charrue devant les boeufs* (reminding us that oxen were the draught animals). Others are less well known, at least nowadays: *comme on dit, à rude asne, rude asnier* (CO 35.504[27-28]) — 'as we say, rude ass, rude owner' (which Littré ascribes to Henri Étienne. I take it to mean 'like dog, like master'. Or again: *c'est saulter du coq a l'asne, comme on dit* (SC VI. p. 13[14]) — 'this is to jump from the cock to the ass, as we say'. But Calvin thinks that this requires explanation, for he adds, 'as we say when we want to finish off one thing by another' (SC VI.13[14-15]).

Far more common, however are the similes. We are not to look in these sermons for the rich imagery of Jeremy Taylor's *Goldengrove Sermons*, even less for the carefully observed images of Shakespeare. Calvin's imagery is commonplace and obvious. He tends to rely on borrowings, and especially borrowings from Scripture. 'Let us learn to submit ourselves wholly to him and not to act like stubborn horses, for it will profit us nothing' (SC V.6[13-14]). '"I know," he says, "what will become of you when you are like fattened horses, resisting me"' (SC VI.180[24-25]). 'We ought to be kept on a tight rein — that is to say, in obedience to God and his Word' (SC VI.184[1-2]). The rebellious horse, the bridle or curb, are derived from such verses as 'Be ye not like to horse and mule, which have no understanding: whose mouth must be kept with bit and bridle, lest they come near unto thee' (BCP: 'fall upon thee') (Ps. 32.9). Allied to these are the images of wild beasts or savage bulls. 'Those who have not received this Word of God act like *bestes saulvages*, their horns levelled against God, their claws against men' (SC VI.56[30-31]).

In our random columns no genuine simile occurs. But if we

turn the page we come upon this: 'when one pricks them they squirt their venom, like the toads they are' (CO 26.167[17-19]). And then this: 'The wicked, as soon as they feel a stroke of the rod from God's hand rebel against him, and if they can escape, they act like a horse that has got its bridle loose and thrown its rider and from rage has gone quite mad, so that no-one can hold it' (CO 26.167[39-44]). And then: 'he sees that [the people] has as it were a mark of ignominy for ever, as if God had branded it' (CO 26.168[5-7]). And then: 'We see that Moses was like a burning fire' (CO 26.169[8-17]). And then: 'if they are not held on a curb, as we say' (CO 26.169[49-50]). And finally: 'On the other hand, if he leaves us without [good leaders] it is as if one were without munitions in a city, so that there is no power, so that there is no defence' (CO 26.170[53-56]).

The simile may be developed into a little character sketch. Thus, on 1 Tim. 4.6 ('nourished up in the words of faith') his imagination enlarges on the word 'nourished': 'Take the case that there is a nurse who is a gossip and a drunkard. Ah well! she can cackle, she can make it look as if the baby is all the world to her. *Mais quoy?* She is just a drunkard, full of intemperance and talk. Instead of sleeping at night, she gives herself up to lechery, so that she has no milk; and the poor child gets no nourishment. She, on the contrary, who will work willingly and yet take substantial nourishment, as well as sleeping properly, she will be able to nourish her baby as well. So is it with those who have to proclaim the Word of God' (CO 53.376[32-45]).

The need for a clearly defined intention in preaching calls up a whole string of images: 'It is like going to a physician and asking for a remedy for a sickness; and if he just talks about his art in general and discusses it, and in the meanwhile the poor sick man gives up the ghost when he could have been restored by prompt treatment — what would have been the good of all the talk? When someone goes to a mason to put some building work in his hands, and he discusses the building of castles and suggests erecting grand buildings in the air, and discusses how he will do it, and pays no attention to the present work, what will come of it? If someone comes to a solicitor [*advocat*] to ask for advice in a lawsuit, and he is going to discuss laws in general without application to the present case — that would be a lot of good! So, then, let us note well that when we treat the Word of God we must have a definite aim and not wander about haphazardly' (Sermon XCV, on Job 26.2-3. CO 34.423^{50}-424^{15}).

It will be seen that all Calvin's images are simple and easily understood. E. Mülhaupt categorises them as military, judicial, natural, animal, artisan, and academic (*Die Predigt Calvins*, 39-63). This is no doubt comprehensive enough, although some are used very much more frequently than others, with, one would guess, the animal occurring most often. but the chief thing to notice about them is their simplicity and familiarity.

The same may be said of his use of homely, every-day expressions, the sort of thing that was the verbal currency of ordinary folk until radio and television enfeebled our language. 'Yes, but this is to bring us to a deeper displeasure with our sins. It often seems to us sufficient to have a good sigh, as one says in common parlance' (CO 35.502$^{2-6}$) — compare the English 'have a good cry'. Or, expounding 1 Tim. 4.8, 'bodily exercise profiteth little': 'Now, he is not talking here about going for a walk, or playing tennis or bowls, or anything of that sort' (CO 53.384$^{9-12}$).

The images and conversation pieces are not without their own humour. But one thing that is totally lacking is the use of anecdotes. We have already heard him saying that they are out of place in the pulpit. The humour tends to be satirical, as one might expect from the author of the *Excuse aux Messieurs les Nicodémites* and *Traicté des Reliques*. 'One does not hear a single word of teaching from [the Pope's] mouth; that would impair his dignity' (CO 54.385$^{19-20}$). Or: 'when women who put on make-up come out into the sun and get hot, the make-up comes off and one see the wrinkles' (CO 53.211$^{1-4}$) — so it is with hypocrites.

Calvin's style as extemporary preacher is markedly different from that which we find in his French writings. There he displays the virtues that make him one of the great French masters and a moulder of modern French. But here, in the sermons, he deliberately adapts his style to the grasp of the common people in his congregation. To use a term that he frequently employs of biblical writers, he 'accommodates' himself to the ignorance of the people. The most marked change is that the conciseness on which he so prided himself has to give place to diffuseness and repetition. Along with these is lost very often the balance of the sentences. Yet it is difficult to think of any other quality that is surrendered. There is still the simplicity and the clarity, the wit and the force, the passion and the high seriousness. To have surrendered them would have meant the surrendering of Calvin himself. Nor should we necessarily think of the style of the sermons as being inferior to that of the considered writings. On the contrary, it is an indication of his mastery in the use of language that he was able to adopt this different style and use it as effectively as the other.

A Chronological Chart

(To give references for each entry would make the chart far too complicated. All the information may be verified from either Raguenier or Colladon in our Appendixes and Bibliographies. The sermons at Church Festivals are printed in italics and placed out of alignment, to indicate that they are interruptions of a series, which, of course, continues after the Festival.)

Morning Sunday	Afternoon	Date	Weekday
Hebrews (cont.) 　*Matthew* 　*Matthew* 　Acts 2 Acts	Psalms (cont.) Ps. 40	1549 Apr. 14 　Apr. 15-19 Apr. 21 - Easter June 9 - Pentecost Aug. 25 Nov. 17 　Dec. 25	Jeremiah (cont.) *Matthew* *Luke*
John *John*		1550 Mar. 30 　Mar. 31-Apr. 5 Apr. 6 - Easter Sept. 6 Nov. 12	 *John* Lamentations Micah
John 18? *John 20. 1ff.?*	Ps. 80.9	1551 　Feb. 6 Feb. 8 Mar. 22 　Mar. 23-28? Mar. 29 - Easter Apr. 2 Sept. 5 Oct. 28	Zephaniah *John 18-19* Hosea Joel Amos
    Acts 16		1552 Feb. 5 Mar. 28 July 18 Nov. 21 Nov. 27	Obadiah Jonah Daniel 5 Ezekiel

A Chronological Chart

Acts (cont.)	Psalms (cont.)	1553	Ezekiel (cont.)
	Ps. 119	Jan. 8	
Passion and Resurrection		Mar. 26	
		Mar. 27 - Apr. 1	*Passion and Resurrection*
Passion and Resurrection		Apr. 2 - Easter	
	Ps. 119	July 2	
Acts 20.17ff.		Sept. 3	
	Ps. 147	Nov. 12	
Luke		Dec. 24 - Christmas	
		1554	
		Feb. 21	Ezekiel (end)
		Feb. 26	Job
Passion and Resurrection		Mar. 18	
		Mar. 21?	*Passion and Resurrection*
Passion and Resurrection		Mar. 25 - Easter	
Morning and Afternoon			
1 Thessalonians			
Acts 2		May 13 - Pentecost	
2 Thessalonians		?	
1 Timothy		Sept. 16	
	Ps. 148	Sept. 30	
Luke		Dec. 23 - Christmas	
		1555	
		Mar. 20	Deuteronomy
Matthew		Apr. 14 - Easter	
1 Timothy (end)	2 Timothy	Apr. 21	
2 Timothy			
Acts 2		June 2	
	Ps. 149	July 4	
Titus		Aug. 18	
1 Corinthians		Oct. 20	
		1556	
		July 15	Deuteronomy (end)
		July 16	Isaiah

1 Corinthians (cont...) 2 Corinthians | Galatians |	Psalms (cont...) Ps. 65	**1557** Feb. 22 Feb. 28 May 30 Aug. 4 Nov. 14 Dec. 31	Isaiah 13 Isaiah 30 Isaiah 42
Ephesians |		**1558** May 15 June 14 Sept. 22	Isaiah 52 Isaiah (vol. 6)
Matthew 28. 1ff. Harmony of Gospels		**1559** Mar. 26 - Easter July Sept. 4	Genesis
Matthew 28.1 ff. *Acts 2. 1-11*	Ps. 46. 1-6 Ps. 46. 7-12 Ps. 48. 2-8 Ps. 48. 9-15	**1560** May 12 May 19 May 26 June 2 - Pentecost June 9	Apr. 14 - Easter
		1561 Feb. 3 Aug. 8	Judges 1 Samuel
Matthew 28?		**1562** Mar. 23 Mar. 28 Mar. 29 - Easter May 23	*Matt. 21.40* to *Matt. 27.66* 2 Samuel
		1563 Feb. 3 ?	2 Samuel (end) 1 Kings
Last Sunday sermon		**1564** Feb. 2 Feb. 6	Last weekday sermon

APPENDIX 1
Catalogues of the Sermons

1. Raguenier-Colladon

In 1557 Raguenier wrote a catalogue of the sermons for which he had been responsible. Thereafter he added to the list year by year. The copy by Colladon in 1564, with the addition of a few glosses, is now in the Archives d'État of Geneva. I translate from SC II. pp. XV-XVII:

Here follows the Catalogue of the Sermons of the late Monsieur Calvin, gathered by the late Maistre Denis Raguenier. The said Catalogue made by Raguenier is here copied by me, N. Colladon, Minister of the Church of Geneva, this year 1564 in the month of September.

Since the penultimate day of September, 1549, I, Denis Raguenier, scribe, have gathered the sermons of Monsieur Calvin and have lodged them in the hands of the Deacons ordained to the oversight of the needs of the poor French who are in the Church of Geneva.

There follow in order:

First, the Sermons preached on Sundays, mornings and afternoons:

On the Acts of the Apostles from the 1st chapter to the 16th, 95 sermons, unbound and not in consecutive order, the first of the said sermons commencing Sunday, 25th day of August, 1549, in the morning.

The said sermons are now bound and make up two volumes.

Item, again on Acts, from the 16th chapter to the end of the book, two volumes bound, of which the first contains 44 sermons and the last 50, making 94 in all, commencing Sunday, 27th day of November, 1552, in the morning.

Item, on the Psalms, 72 sermons preached at various times; unbound and not consecutive, owing to my being taken ill; commencing Sunday, 17th day of November in the same year 1549, afternoon.

Item, on the *Octonaires* [= eight-verse stanzas] of Psalm 119, 22 sermons, which have been printed; commencing Sunday, 8th day of January, 1553.

Item, on the two Epistles of St Paul to the Thessalonians, 46 sermons, consecutive and following one after the other; commencing Sunday, 26th [=25th] day of March, 1554, afternoon.

Item, on the 1st Epistle of St Paul to Timothy, 55 sermons bound in one volume, consecutive and following one after the other; commencing Sunday, 16th day of September, 1554 in the morning.

Item, on the 2nd Epistle of St Paul to Timothy, 31 sermons, and on the Epistle to Titus 17, making in all 48 sermons, following one after the other, commencing Sunday, 21st day of April, 1555, in the morning.

Item, on the 1st Epistle of St Paul to the Corinthians, 110 sermons in two volumes, the first containing 58 sermons and the last 52, following one after another in order, and commencing Sunday 20th day of October, 1555 in the morning.

Item, on the 2nd Epistle of St Paul to the Corinthians, 66 sermons, bound in one volume and following one after another in order, commenced Sunday, the last day of February, 1557.

Item, on the Epistle to the Galatians, 43 sermons, bound in one volume and following one after another; commenced Sunday, 14th day of November, 1557, afternoon.

Item, on the Epistle of St Paul to the Ephesians, 48 sermons, bound in one volume, following and consecutive one after another; commenced the 15th day of May, 1558, Sunday afternoon.

There follow the sermons preached on the other days of the week:

First, on the book of the revelations of the Prophet Jeremiah, 91 sermons supplied at the hands of M. de Normandie

Appendix 1

(as also the underwritten), the said sermons not bound and not following one after another; commencing the first of them Tuesday, 12th day of November, 1549.

Item, on the Lamentations of Jeremiah, 25 sermons, following one after another and bound in one volume; commenced Saturday, 6th day of September, 1550.

Item, on the Prophet Micah, 28 sermons, following in order, bound in one volume; commenced Wednesday, 12th day of November, 1550.

Item, on the Prophet Zephaniah, 17 sermons, also following and consecutive the one after the other, bound in one volume; commenced Friday, 6th day of the month February, 1551.

Item, on the Prophet Hosea, 65 sermons, bound in one volume, following and consecutive in order; commenced Thursday, 2nd day of April, 1551.

Item, on the Prophet Joel, 17 sermons, following one after another in order and bound in one volume; commencing Saturday, 5th day of September, 1551.

Item, on the Prophet Amos, 43 sermons following and consecutive, contained in one volume, and commenced Wednesday, 28th day of October, 1551.

Item, 5 sermons on the vision of Obadiah; commencing the 5th day of February, 1552.

Item, the first 6 sermons preached on the Prophet Jonah; commencing Monday, 28th of March, 1552, bound in the volume with Zephaniah and Obadiah. And as for the rest of Jonah and the prophet Nahum, together with the first four chapters of the Prophet Daniel, they were not recorded, owing to my being taken ill.

Item, on the Prophet Daniel, commencing at the 5th chapter to the end, 47 sermons, following in order, and bound in one volume; commenced Monday, 18th day of July, 1552.

Item, on the Prophet Ezekiel, 174 sermons comprising three volumes; that is, the first containing 56 sermons, the second 50, and the third and last 69, following and consecutive in order; commenced Monday, 21st day of November, 1552.

Item, on the book entitled Job, 159 sermons comprising three volumes; that is, the first containing 56 sermons, the second 62, and the third and last 41, following and consecutive one after another; commenced Monday, 26th day of February, 1554.

Item, on the 5th book of Moses called Deuteronomy, 200 sermons contained in three volumes; that is, the first containing 62 sermons, the second 68, and the third and last 71, also consecutive and without a gap; commenced Wednesday, 20th day of March, 1555.

Item, on the Prophet Isaiah, which was treated in this present year 1557; the first volume containing 66 sermons, following and consecutive; commenced Thursday, 16th day of July, 1556.

Item, the second volume on the Prophet Isaiah, containing 66 sermons; commenced Monday, 22nd day of February, 1557.

Item, the third volume on the Prophet Isaiah, containing 67 sermons; commenced Wednesday, 4th day of August, 1557.

Item, the fourth volume on the Prophet Isaiah, containing 57 sermons; commenced Wednesday, last day of December, 1558.

Item, the fifth volume on the Prophet Isaiah, containing 44 sermons following and consecutive in order; commenced Tuesday, 14th day of June, 1558.

Item, the sixth and final volume on the Prophet Isaiah, containing 43 sermons, also following and consecutive one after another; commenced Thursday, 22nd day of September, 1558. The number of the said sermons on Isaiah contained in six volumes specified above comes in all to 343 sermons.

Item, the first volume on the first book of Moses called Genesis, containing 61 sermons, following and consecutive one after another; commenced Monday, 4th day of September, 1559.

Item, the second volume on the said book of Genesis, containing 62 sermons, following and consecutive; commenced Wednesday, 21st day of February, 1560.

A few observations on this Catalogue.

First, although the indications of sermons not being consecutive are to be heeded, the absence of such a note should not be taken as meaning that the sermons are not consecutive. Raguenier seems to add the note as and when he likes. (He also

Appendix 1 157

seems to see a distinction between 'following' and 'consecutive'.)

It is also clear that there are several slips in the list. Those that I have noticed are: 55 sermons on 1 Timothy and 31 on 2 Timothy, instead of 54 and 30; 2 Timothy began on Sunday afternoon, not morning, according to my calculations; the numbers he gives for Ezekiel add up to 175, not 174; similarly, those for Deuteronomy come to 201, instead of the 200 it should be.

It is not quite easy to reckon up the number of volumes involved. Those which are definitely said to have been bound are: Acts, 4 volumes; 1 Timothy, 1 volume; 1 and 2 Corinthians, 3 volumes; Galatians, 1 volume, as also Ephesians; Lamentations, 1 volume; Micah, 1 volume; Zephaniah, Obadiah, and Jonah, 1 volume; Hosea 1 volume; Joel, Amos, and Daniel, 1 volume each; Ezekiel, 3 volumes; Job, 3 volumes; Isaiah, 6 volumes; and Genesis, 2 volumes. This gives 31 volumes. But to these we should add, as probably bound, 1 and 2 Thessalonians, 1 volume; 2 Timothy and Titus, 1 volume; making 33 bound volumes. The loose sheets are: Psalms; Psalm 119; Jeremiah. Taking each of these as equivalent to one volume, we have 36 volumes.

The individual sermons are easier to number, and I make it 2,040.

We must remember that this Catalogue includes (apart from Genesis) only sermons recorded by Raguenier. It therefore does not include the Harmony of the Gospels or the *Plusieurs Sermons* on Sundays, or Judges, 1 and 2 Samuel, or 1 Kings.

2. The Catalogue of 1697

We have mentioned that, when the manuscripts were transferred to the care of the library, they were not included in the next catalogue. That of 1697 is therefore the first catalogue after Raguenier's own, one hundred and forty years earlier. It is merely a list:

        Genesis   2 volumes

2 Samuel	1 volume
1 Kings	1 volume
Psalms	3 volumes
Isaiah	6 volumes
Jeremiah	7 volumes
Ezekiel	7 volumes
Daniel	2 volumes
Hosea	2 volumes
Joel	1 volume
Amos	1 volume
Micah	2 volumes
Obadiah and Jonah	1 volume
Zephaniah	1 volume
Harmony of Gospels	1 volume
Acts	4 volumes
1 Corinthians	2 volumes
2 Corinthians	1 volume
1 and 2 Thessalonians	1 volume
Hebrews	1 volume
History of Nativity, Passion, and Resurrection of Jesus Christ, and on Acts 2	1 volume

The positive side of this list is that it confirms the existence in 1697 of the post-1560 sermons. It is also quite in order that some sets should now be omitted. 1 and 2 Timothy and Titus had been printed, as also Deuteronomy, Job, Galatians, and Ephesians; and no doubt the printer would have disposed of the manuscripts after the printing — either by destroying them or using some of the sheets for binding.

For the rest, however, the figures should be treated very sceptically. There could not have been seven volumes for Jeremiah. The seven ascribed to Ezekiel consisted of two separate copies, as the new catalogue in 1702 makes clear; Zephaniah, Obadiah, and Jonah were, according to Raguenier, all in one volume, not two. We have no record that the series on Hebrews was recorded; it is not in Raguenier's Catalogue.

The reason why Daniel, Psalm 119, and the *Plusieurs Sermons* are included in spite of the fact that they had been printed is probably because these manuscripts were not Raguenier's originals but copies that had been made.

We may therefore disregard the figure of 48 volumes. It is rather surprising to me that attempts have been made to rationalise the list, which is not without value for confirmation of some points but has very little worth in details.

3. The Catalogue of 1779

In his *Catalogue raisonné des manuscrits conservés dans la Bibliothèque... de Genève* (1779), Jean Senebier, the Librarian, puts the number of volumes at 44. Yet the manuscript copy of his book makes it 39. Moreover, the sets which had been printed are brought back into the list, together with the erroneous numbers of sermons given by Raguenier.

Genesis	123 Sermons in 2 volumes
Deuteronomy	200 Sermons in 4 volumes
Job	159 Sermons in 3 volumes
Psalms	72 Sermons in 2 volumes
Isaiah	43 Sermons in 7 volumes
Jeremiah	91 Sermons in 2 volumes
Lamentations	25 Sermons in 1 volume
Ezekiel	174 Sermons in 4 volumes
Daniel	47 Sermons in 1 volume
Hosea	65 Sermons in 1 volume
Joel	17 Sermons in 1 volume
Amos	43 Sermons in 1 volume
Obadiah	5 Sermons in 1 volume
Jonah	6 Sermons in 1 volume
Micah	28 Sermons in 1 volume
Zephaniah	17 Sermons in 1 volume
Acts	189 Sermons in 3 volumes
1 Corinthians	110 Sermons in 2 volumes
2 Corinthians	66 Sermons in 1 volume
Galatians	43 Sermons in 1 volume
1 and 2 Thessalonians	46 Sermons in 1 volume
1 Timothy	55 Sermons in 1 volume
2 Timothy	31 Sermons in 1 volume
Titus	48 Sermons in 1 volume

It is impossible to take these numbers, any more than those in the 1697 Catalogue, as providing a reliable account of the state of the manuscript collection at the time. I will refrain from pointing out the errors and discrepancies, for the reader will easily supply them himself from Raguenier's Catalogue.

4. List of Sermons on Church Festivals

(Professor Bernard Gagnebin, when Librarian of the Bibliothèque publique et universitaire, unearthed the following list (ms. fr. 30) of the contents of a volume of Festival sermons preached in Geneva. It contained thirty-four sermons by Calvin and fifteen by Viret. The sermons themselves were missing. I am grateful to Professor Gagnebin for sending me, many years ago, a photocopy of ms. fr. 30. Professor Mülhaupt has discussed (in SC VII. pp. XLVIIff.) the difficult relationship of these sermons with those published in *Plusieurs sermons.*)

Table of the Sermons contained in this present Volume.

First, seven sermons made on the story of the passion and resurrection of our Lord Jesus Christ according to St Matthew; commenced Sunday — day of April, 1549, and ended the following Sunday, the 21st of the said month of April, in the said year 1549; arranged numerically — 1, 2, 3, 4, 5, 6, 7.

Item, another sermon, of Sunday, 9th day of June, 1549, the day of Pentecost; made on the 2nd chapter of the Acts of the Apostles.

The aforesaid sermons gathered [= recorded] by M. André de la Chesnaye.

Item, another sermon, made on Wednesday, 25th day of December, 1550 [= 1549], the day of the Christmas Lord's Supper. On the story of the Nativity of our Lord Jesus Christ according to St Luke. Number 9.

Item, eight other sermons, following the one after the other, made on the story of the passion and resurrection of our Lord Jesus Christ according to St John; commenced Sunday, the last day but one of March and ended on the following Sunday, 6th

Appendix 1

day of April, 1550; arranged numerically — 10, 11, 12, 13, 14, 15, 16, 17.

Item, another sermon, of Wednesday, 25th day of March, 1551, made on the story of the passion of our Lord, according to St John chapters 18 and 19. Number 18.

Item, eight other sermons, following one after the other, made on the story of the passion and resurrection of our Lord; commenced Sunday, 26th day of March and ended the following Sunday, 2nd of April, 1553; arranged numerically — 19, 20, 21, 22, 23, 24, 25, 26.

Item, another sermon made on Sunday, 24th day of December, 1554 [= 1553], on the story of the Nativity of our Lord according to St Luke. Number 27.

Item, three other sermons, made on the story of the passion and resurrection of our Lord; commenced Sunday, 18th March and ended Sunday, 25th day of the said month of March, 1554; arranged numerically — 28, 29, 30.

Item, another sermon, on Sunday, 13th day of May, 1554, the day of the Pentecost Lord's Supper; made on the 2nd chapter of the Acts of the Apostles. Number 31.

Item, another sermon, made on Sunday, 23rd day of December, 1555 [= 1554], the day of the Christmas Lord's Supper; on the story of the Nativity of our Lord according to St Luke. Number 32.

Item, another sermon, on Sunday, 14th day of April, 1555, the day of the Easter Lord's Supper; made on the story of the resurrection of our Lord according to St Matthew. Number 33.

Item, another sermon, on Sunday, 2nd day of June, 1555, the day of the Pentecost Lord's Supper; made on the 2nd chapter of the Acts. Number 34.

The said sermons made by M. Jehan Calvin, Minister of the Holy Gospel of our Lord in the Church of Geneva, and gathered by Denis Raguenier of Bar-sur-Seine.

This list calls for one or two comments.

(1) On three occasions Calvin preached a number of sermons from the Sunday next before Easter to Easter Day; in 1549 seven and in 1550 and 1553 eight. These were always on the Passion and Resurrection from Matthew, Luke, or John.

The course therefore entailed either two sermons on each of the two Sundays and three or four during the week, or, if the Sunday afternoons were devoted to the Psalter, one sermon each Sunday and five, or six, on the weekdays. The latter is perhaps the more probable.

(2) Sermon 18 is assigned to the one day, Wednesday, March 25; but it is given as text John chapters 18 and 19, comprising eighty-two verses. This is so highly improbable, that we must conjecture that there were originally seven sermons on John 18-19 and (on Easter Day) one on John 20.1ff.

(3) Similarly with Sermons 28, 29, 30. Here we are given no precise text; but the formula 'passion and resurrection of our Lord' refers in other entries to two or three chapters (very long chapters in Matthew and Luke).

(4) From the evidence contained in this list it seems a fair inference that Calvin was accustomed to break off the series which he was preaching in order to give up Holy Week and Easter to 'l'hystoire de la passion et resurrection de nostre Seigneur', and that he observed Whit Sunday in the same manner with a sermon, usually on Acts 2, and Christmas Day (or the Sunday next before Christmas) with a sermon on the Nativity — all those that we have or know of are on Luke. Easter, Whit, and Christmas were, of course, three of the four Communion Sundays.

(5) Raguenier always reckoned Christmas Day as belonging to the following year. We have brought this into line with our own practice.

APPENDIX 2
Dating the Sermons on 1 and 2 Timothy and Job

The Sermons in manuscript, those in *Supplementa Calviniana* and in some early printed editions carry the date on which each sermon was preached. Unfortunately, not all the early editions followed this helpful practice. Those on the Pastoral Epistles and Job are among the delinquents. With these three, however, it is very important to know the precise dates, because of the crisis in Church affairs in Geneva. Many of the statements made in Chapter 8 were only possible because I worked out the date of each sermon.

The first step is to take the starting date of a series as supplied by Raguenier in his Catalogue and copied by Colladon into his *Vie de Calvin*. Leaving Job to a little later, we see that 1 Timothy began on Sunday morning, September 16, 1554.

The second step is to fix the *terminus ad quem*. And here we learn from Raguenier-Colladon that 2 Timothy was started on 'Sunday, 21st day of April, 1555, in the morning'. We shall have to correct the time of day; but for the moment all we need is that 1 Timothy ended on or before April 21, 1555.

To fill in the dates of 1 Timothy we turn first to internal evidence. These are Sunday sermons and therefore usually went in pairs, one in the morning and one in the afternoon. It was Calvin's frequent (but not invariable) custom to refer in the afternoon sermon to something he had said in the morning, with some such formula as 'we heard this morning...' or 'St Paul told us this morning...' Occasionally also, but rather less often, he will promise to carry on with an unfinished point 'apres disner'. If we note these places we are able to couple various sermons as belonging together on one Sunday.

The 1 Timothy sermons referring back to 'ce matin' are: 2, 4, 7, 9, 15, 17, 21, 23, 25, 27, 30, 32, 34, 38, 46, 50, 52. We therefore assign complete Sundays to 1-2/ 3-4/ 6-7/ 8-9/ 14-15/ 16-17/ 20-21/ 22-23/ 24-25/ 26-27/ 29-30/ 31-32/ 33-34/ 37-38/ 45-46/ 49-50/ 51-52.

Those looking forward to 'apres disner' are: 12, 20, 35. We therefore add to our list numbers 12-13/ 35-36 (20-21 we have already). It is true that looking forward is less certain than looking back. Some emergency might have prevented him from preaching in the afternoon. But in fact the final arrangement of the sermons will show that this is a groundless fear.

We still have sixteen sermons unaccounted for, some of which (e.g. number 5) stand on their own without any hope of a partner. It is now necessary to look for external evidence.

We know that Calvin sometimes interrupted a series to preach on a psalm in the afternoon. Moreover, we have Colladon's list of special sermons preached on certain feasts of the Church (Appendix 1, 4). From these two sources we find that on September 30, 1554, the afternoon sermon was on Psalm 148; that on December 23 a Christmas sermon was preached on Luke 2 in the morning; and that on April 14, 1555, being Easter Day, Calvin preached on Matthew 28. These will provide partners for three of the unattached, leaving thirteen.

The number of Sundays between September 16 and April 21 (when 2 Timothy began) is thirty-two; which gives sixty-four preaching times. But there are only fifty-four sermons — or rather, fifty-five, counting the first on 2 Timothy if it was preached on the afternoon of April 21. We have several Sundays over, therefore. But three of these can be disposed of at once, for the Registres du Conseil show that Calvin was in Bern on the Sundays March 10 and 31, and April 7.

To return to a piece of internal evidence. February 3 was the date of the first day of the fateful elections mentioned earlier. As we saw, Calvin referred to the elections as taking place 'today, and tomorrow, and tomorrow'. This in Sermon 39. Sermon 39, therefore, fell on February 3.

Appendix 2 165

We can now arrange the sermons from September 16 to February 3. 1-2/ 3-4/ 5- Ps. 148/6-7/ 8-9/ 10-11/ 12-13/ 14-15/ 16-17/ 18-19/ 20-21/ 22-23/ 24-25/ 26-27/ Luke 2-28/ 29-30/ 31-32/ 33-34/ 35-36/ 37-38/ 39.

From February 3 to April 21, the matter becomes more difficult. Assuming that Sermon 39 was preached on the morning of February 3 and not in the afternoon, we are left with twenty-two preaching times from the afternoon of February 3 to the morning of April 21. For three Sundays he was at Bern, so that we subtract six from the twenty-two, and on Easter morning there was a special sermon; so that fifteen preaching times are left. But from Sermon 40 to Sermon 54 there are fifteen sermons. We therefore conclude that the sermons must have been preached on the days and at the times to which we have assigned them.

The following chart will demonstrate this clearly. The references to 'ce matin' and apres disner' are all to CO 53. For interest I have also included (in italics) weddings and baptisms; and here the references are to CO 21.

1 Timothy 1554-1555
(*=ce matin; †=apres disner. I have placed weddings and baptisms in the morning where the Registres give no indication of time.)

Date		a.m.	References, etc.	p.m.	References, etc.
Sept.	16	1		2	* CO 53. 17[19]
	23	3		4	* CO 53. 41[1]
	30	5		Ps. 148	SC VII. p. VII
Oct.	7	6	*wedding* CO 21.587	7	* CO 53. 83[2,3]
	14	8		9	* CO 53. 99[44]
	21	10		11	*2 weddings* CO 21. 587
	28	12	† CO 53.148[15] *wedding* CO 21.588	13	
Nov.	4	14		15	* CO 53. 171[1]
	11	16		17	* CO 53. 197[1]
	18	18	*wedding* CO 21. 589	19	
	25	20	† CO 53. 243[15]	21	* CO 53. 245[1]
Dec.	2	22	*wedding* CO 21. 590	23	* CO 53. 274[2]
	9	24	*wedding* CO 21. 590	25	* CO 53. 293[8]

Dec.	16	26	*baptism* CO 21. 591	27	* CO 53. 317[18]
	23	Luke 2	SC VII.p.XLVIII	28	
	30	29		30	*CO 53. 355[45]
Jan.	6	31	*wedding* CO 21. 592	32	* CO 53. 381[38]
	13	33		34	* CO 53. 405[23]
	20	35	† CO 53. 428[30]	36	*wedding* (or a.m. CO 21. 593)
	27	37		38	* CO 53. 458[11]
Feb.	3	39	elections CO 53. 475[45ff]	40	
	10	41	2 *weddings* CO 21. 594	42	
	17	43	3 *weddings* CO 21. 595	44	
	24	45	*wedding* CO 21. 595	46	* CO 53. 545[1]
Mar.	3	47	*wedding* CO 21. 596	48	
	10	-	in Bern CO 21. 596, 597	-	
	17	49		50	* CO 53. 593[43]
	24	51	2 *weddings* (?) CO 21. 600	52	* CO 53. 619[23]
	31	-	in Bern CO 21. 600	-	
Apr.	7	-	in Bern CO. 21. 600	-	
	14	Matt.28	SC VII. p. XLVIII	53	
	21	54			

We proceed to 2 *Timothy*, which we have shown to have begun on the afternoon of April 21, not morning, as the Raguenier Catalogue. Our task is here made rather more difficult in that we are not given a date for the beginning of *Titus*. Hence we must deal at first with 2 *Timothy* and *Titus* together.

The series on 1 Corinthians began on October 20. Therefore we may expect *Titus* to have ended on either the afternoon of October 13 or the morning of October 20. If we first assume the former, it will give us twenty-six Sundays, fifty-two preaching times. But there are forty-seven sermons. Therefore, five preaching times have to be accounted for. One, April 21 in the morning, has been settled, leaving us only four. Two of these present no difficulty. June 2 was Whit Sunday; in the morning Calvin preached on Acts 2. And in the afternoon of July 14 he preached on Psalm 149. So there are only two left idle.

Appendix 2

When we apply the '*ce matin*' and '*apres disner*' tests to *2 Timothy* we find that Sermons 3, 5, 7, 9, 12, 14, 17, 21, 24, and 26 use the former and 4, 10, 16, and 27 the latter. So we have the pairs: 2-3/ 4-5/ 6-7/ 8-9/ 10-11/ 11-12/ 13-14/ 16-17/ 20-21/ 23-24/ 25-26/ 27-28. The anomaly of 10-11/ 11-12 is easily cleared up; Sermons 10 and 11 were preached on May 26 (as we shall see) and Sermon 12 on the afternoon of Whit Sunday. The three references to '*ce matin*' in it all concern things he had said about the Holy Spirit in his Whit Sunday sermon in the morning.

For *Titus* the '*ce matin*' sermons are 2, 4, 8, 11, 13, 15; and the sole '*apres disner*' one is 5. Hence the pairs: 1-2/ 3-4/ 5-6/ 7-8/ 10-11/ 12-13/ 14-15.

The sermons in *2 Timothy* which are unpaired are 1, 15, 18, 19, 22, 29, 30. Of these, the first is already placed and four others fall into pairs — 18-19/ 29-30. Number 22 will pair with Psalm 149.

Those unpaired in *Titus* are 9, 16, 17, which will fall into place as 16-17, leaving 9 on its own.

We need not worry overmuch to have *2 Timothy* 15 and *Titus* 9 unaccounted for. The former must fall on June 16, the latter on September 15. The reason for September 15 is not too difficult to seek. No mention is made in Raguenier or Colladon of the final psalm in the Psalter. Calvin preached on Ps. 148 on September 30, 1554, and on Ps. 149 on July 14, 1555. I would therefore assign Ps. 150 to September 15, 1555. But for June 16 I can offer no firm suggestion. The Registers tell us that on that day 'Calvin married four couples in St Pierre' (CO 21.609). May it be that he then preached a wedding sermon which went unrecorded or has been lost? But he had three weddings on June 9 and still preached twice. Or was it that four weddings was too much even for him, and he did not preach? However that may be, it is hard to see how the sermons on 2 Timothy and Titus can be arranged any differently from the following charts. Confirmation is afforded by *Two godly sermons* (1576), in which Sermon IV (2 Tim. 1.8-9) is assigned to 'Sondaye the v. of may 1555, in the forenone' and Sermon V (2 Tim. 1.8-10) to 'Sonday the v. of maye 1555, after dyner'.

2 Timothy 1555

Date		a.m.	References, etc.	p.m.	References, etc.
Apr.	21	-		1	
	28	2		3	* CO 54. 31[22]
May	5	4	† CO 54. 52[30-31]	5	* CO 54. 51[34]
	12	6		7	* CO 54. 77[1]
	19	8	wedding CO 21. 605	9	* CO 54. 103[1]
	26	10	† CO 54. 125[8-9]	11	
June	2	Acts 2	SC VII. p. XLVIII. Whit.	12	* CO 54. 145[16]
	9	13	3 Weddings CO 21. 608	14	* CO 54. 163[45]
	16	15	4 weddings CO 21. 609	?	
	23	16	† CO 54. 197[36] wedding CO 21. 609	17	* CO 54. 197[40]
	30	18	2 weddings CO 21. 610	19	
July	7	20		21	* CO 54. 256[31]
	14	22		Ps. 149	SC VII.p. VII
	21	23		24	* CO 54. 285[38]
	28	25	wedding CO 21. 611	26	* CO 54. 307[37]
Aug.	4	27	† CO 54. 332[19] wedding CO 21. 611	28	
	11	29		30	

Titus 1555

Date		a.m.	References, etc.	p.m.	References, etc.
Aug.	18	1		2	* CO 54. 391[1]
	25	3		4	* CO 54. 417[1]
Sept.	1	5	† CO 54. 442 [14-15]	6	
	8	7		8	* CO 54. 469[21]
	15	9		Ps. 150?	
	22	10		11	* CO 54. 509[12]
	29	12		13	* CO 54. 535[22]
Oct.	6	14		15	* CO 54. 561[21]
	13	16		17	

The attempt to assign precise dates to the sermons on Job seems doomed to failure. In theory (that is, according to the regulations) Calvin preached each weekday of alternate weeks. In practice, as we see from the dated sermons on Deuter-

Appendix 2

onomy, the pattern often was of five sermons from Monday to Friday of alternate weeks with a sermon on the intervening Wednesday. Whether the same holds good for *Job* we do not know. But even if this seems a slight difficulty, in that it would only affect every sixth sermon as to whether it was preached on a Saturday or the following Wednesday, yet there are insufficient references to 'yesterday' (analogous to the Sunday 'this morning' and 'after dinner') for us to be able to set the whole series out in order. Indeed only in one place (of an admittedly not meticulous search of the 159 sermons) could I construct a full week out of the references (Sermons 49-54). Once there is a series of five sermons, four times a series of four; but most often only pairs.

Nor are we any further forward by reckoning that there were one hundred and sixty-eight preaching days and only one hundred and fifty-nine sermons. Calvin was in Bern for some of those days, but we do not know how many.

The best we can do is to observe that, if *Deuteronomy* began on Wednesday, March 20, 1555, with the second sermon on the following Monday, we should expect the last sermon of *Job* to have fallen on the Friday or Saturday preceding March 20; that is, March 15 or 16. The week March 11-16 comes, in fact, in the correct sequence of alternate weeks reckoning from February 26, 1554.

Between the start of *Job* and the start of *1 Timothy* there were fifteen preaching weeks, and from then until the beginning of *Deuteronomy* thirteen preaching weeks. As a rough guide, then, we may reckon that somewhere between Sermons 85 and 90 of *Job* coincided with the opening of *1 Timothy*. It is, of course, not impossible that the first visit to Bern accounted for most of the nine missing days, and that our figures are more accurate than I fear.

There is little point in trying to arrange these sermons in a chart as we have done with the Pastoral Epistles; but the following assignment into weeks may not be too far out and may conceivably be useful:

September	24-29	Sermons	91-96
October	8-13	Sermons	97-101
	22-27	Sermons	102-106

November	5-10	Sermons 107-111
	19-24	Sermons 112-117
December	3-8	Sermons 118-123
	17-22	Sermons 124-129
December 31-January 5		Sermons 130-135
January	14-19	Sermons 136-141
January	28-February 2	Sermons 142-147
February	11-16	Sermons 148-153
February	25-March 2	Sermons 154-159

(Some time after making the above calculations and writing the rather pessimistic view of the possibilities, I had occasion, in compiling the Bibliography, to study more carefully the details of ms. fr. 40a. I see that the two sermons on Job mentioned there bear precise dates. The sermon on Job 33.17ff. is no doubt Sermon 125 (although the text as given in CO is 33.18-25), which is dated as Tuesday, December 18. That on Job 33.20-34.3 will be Sermon 128 (CO gives the text as 33.29-34.3), and this is dated Friday, December 21. The reader will see that I had assigned Sermons 124-129 to the week of Monday, December 17. For this week, at least, my calculation was precisely correct. There seems, therefore, a fair probability that the other dates in the list are correct or not very far wrong.

I have left the whole passage I wrote unchanged, to show that the line of argument I have adopted with all three series yields sound results.)

From the indeterminateness of Job it is refreshing to turn to the precise dating of Deuteronomy, given at the head of each sermon. There is no need to do more, then, than to set out the chart which follows, showing the relationship in time between these sermons and those on 1 and 2 Timothy.

Appendix 2

1 and 2 Timothy and Deuteronomy 1555
(The Festival references are to chapters, the ordinary to sermon numbers.)

Sundays	Sermons			Weekdays		Sermons	
Mar. 17	49	1 Timothy	50	Mar.	20	Deut.	1
24	51		52		25, 27		2 - 3
31		in Bern					
Apr. 7		in Bern		Apr.	11 - 13		4 - 6
14	*Matt. 28.*		1 Tim. 53		17		7
21	1 Tim. 54.		2 Tim. 1		22 - 26		8 - 12
28	2	2 Timothy	3	May	1		13
May 5	4		5		6 - 10		14 - 18
12	6		7		15		19
19	8		9		20 - 24		20 - 24
26	10		11		29		25
June 2	*Acts 2*		12	June	3 - 7		26 - 30
9	13		14		12		31
16	15		?		17 - 21		32 - 35
23	16		17		26		36
30	18		19	July	1 - 5		37 - 41
July 7	20		21				
14	22		Ps. 149		16 - 20		42 - 46
21	23		24		24		47
28	25		26		29-Aug. 3		48 - 53
Aug. 4	27		28		7		54
11	29		30		12ff.		55ff.

APPENDIX 3

The Biblical Text

We have said that 'when preaching on the Old Testament Calvin translated his text direct from the Hebrew', and that from this it may be deduced that he translated from the Greek for his New Testament sermons. But it must be made clear at the outset that for various reasons which will emerge we cannot reach such a firm conclusion on the New Testament as with *Isaiah*. We may, however, suggest a probable line of argument that will leave us with some assurance of its validity.

We begin with an outline of the arguments put forward in the Introduction to the sermons on Isaiah 30-41 (SC III.).

There were at Calvin's disposal when preaching on Isaiah Bibles in Hebrew, Greek, Latin, and French. Since he was speaking in French to a French-speaking congregation, we should expect him to use a French Bible, probably one of those printed in Geneva and in the revision of which he had had a hand. In fact, the text in *Isaiah* is not to be found in any French Bible printed up to the date of the sermons, 1556ff. We may take it, then, that he did not use a French Bible when preaching on Isaiah.

The Greek Old Testament is also to be ruled out because, where it differs from the Hebrew, Calvin's text does not agree with it. We must also say in general that he treated the Septuagint rather as an interesting variant than as an authoritative source.

Since he lectured and wrote many books in Latin, then, if his text was not taken from the French, it would be reasonable to

Appendix 3

suppose that he translated his text from a Latin Bible. The objections to this are that he had a very poor view of the Vulgate (see his strictures on it in *Acta Synodi Tridentinae cum Antidoto*, CO 7.411ff.). Moreover, the available alternative versions do not match his French text consistently.

We are left with the fourth possibility, the Hebrew. This may seem surprising; but we learn from a contemporary source that in lecturing, Calvin 'first recited each verse in Hebrew and then turned it into Latin' (CO 40.23-24). If he was a good enough Hebraist to do this in his lectures, then he was capable of doing it in the sermons as well.

Confirmation is afforded by a comparison of texts repeated at the head of a succeeding sermon. It shows us that the repetitions usually introduce variants from the first. For example, at the head of Sermon XX Isa. 33.21 reads (translating literally): 'For the Lord *is excellent* among us'. For Sermon XXI this becomes: 'The Lord *will be exalted* among us'. The meaning is unchanged; the Hebrew has simply been rendered slightly differently. Or Isa. 33.24 is translated as 'Je suis *infirmé* for Sermon XX, but as 'Je suis *debilé* for Sermon XXI. Comparison of some French renderings with the Hebrew show that where the Hebrew is straightforward, the repetitions tend to vary little if at all; when difficulties appeared, the differences were marked, as we should expect from extemporary translating.

Taking all these considerations into account, it is hard to see how one can escape the conclusion that Calvin used a Hebrew Bible when preaching on Isaiah.

When, however, we come to our other special series we are unable to apply the same arguments. For one thing, *Deuteronomy, Job* and *1 and 2 Timothy* do not exist in manuscript but only in printed copies. We have therefore to go elsewhere for our evidence. *Isaiah* contains the four sermons on chapter 38.4-20, Hezekiah's song after his sickness. Professor F. M. Higman has collated the relevant pages of ms. fr. 18 with the 1562 printed text and has found a large number of alterations, intended to make the spoken word more congenial to readers. For the Biblical text the alterations were light; for example, 'when he was sick and healed' (v. 4) became the more correct 'when he had been sick and was healed'. But textual criticism lives on details and the slightest alteration to a text makes precise comparison impossible. Therefore, where we possess only a printed copy of a series and not also the manuscript, we cannot be sure that we have the Biblical text as Calvin spoke it; in fact, we can be fairly certain that we do not have it. To establish that such and such a printed text corresponded to some printed Bible would merely indicate that an editor or printer had used that Bible for the purpose. This is why we cannot apply the arguments used for *Isaiah* to *Deuteronomy, Job,* and *1 and 2 Timothy,* which all remain only in printed copies.

We may, of course, infer that what is true of *Isaiah* will also be true of the other Old Testament sermons, inasmuch as there seems no good reason why Calvin should have adopted this practice for *Isaiah* alone. Nevertheless, it will not be possible to verify this by the methods of textual criticism.

For the New Testament sermons the question becomes whether Calvin used a French, Latin, or Greek New Testament. For the reasons given earlier, we may rule out the possibility that Calvin now used a Latin Bible. We are therefore left with French and Greek.

We may assume that the manuscript was tidied up for the printed edition. But this fact may also be turned to our advantage; for it means that any discrepancies between the main text in one sermon and the same main text used in a subsequent sermon must have different sources — either they come from different French Bibles or the one comes from a French Bible and the other from Calvin himself. The latter is the more probable.

Let us examine two examples of these doublets. (And I am grateful to Professor Higman for sending me photocopies of some pages of 1 and 2 Timothy.)

1. 1 Tim. 3.1-4 is the main text for Sermons XX, XXI, and XXII. They are identical. Verses 3-4 also occur as part of the main text of Sermon XXIII; they, too, are identical with the others. It is therefore clear either that, if this is Calvin's own text, he was reading from a French Bible or that the editor has substituted the text of a French Bible for Calvin's original version.

2. 2 Tim. 2.22-26 (Sermon XVI), 2.23-26 (Sermon XVII),

Appendix 3 175

and 2.25-26 (Sermon XVIII) present a rather different picture. Although for Sermons XVI and XVII the words are identical, apart from v. 26, where XVII has *pris* for *prins* (without significance for our purposes), Sermon XVIII is different.

Sermon XVI & XVII	**Sermon XVIII**
	Il faut que le serviteur du Seigneur
enseignant avec douceur	enseigne patiemment
ceux qui resistent,	ceux qui resistent,
pour essayer si quelquefois	ascavoir-mon si en quelque temps
Dieu leur donnera repentance	Dieu leur donnera repentance

We cannot regard the alterations as editorial because, although an editor could well have supplied 'Il faut que le serviteur du Seigneur' from v. 24 and turned 'enseignant' into 'enseigne', he needed thereafter only to continue to copy the Bible before him with 'avec douceur . . .' I reconstruct what happened as follows: The trouble for the editor began with the fact that the text for Sermon XVIII started in the middle of a verse and he could not simply continue with the present participle 'teaching'. He therefore reverted to what was written in the manuscript (i.e. Calvin's own version, in which he makes a new sentence begin with one of his customary formulae, 'Il faut que' . . .). But the editor then went on copying the manuscript a little longer than he needed to before he remembered and switched back to the printed Bible with 'Dieu leur donnera . . .' That in fact we have Calvin's own version here is confirmed by his twice quoting the verse in this form — not in Sermon XVIII but in XVII, where it does not, of course, match the main text: '"Ascavoir", dit-il, "si Dieu leur donnera . . ."' (CO 54.206[9-10]); and 'Saint Paul notamment dit, Ascavoir-mon si quelquefois Dieu leur donnera . . .' (CO 54.207[19-21]).

There are therefore strong indications that for *1 and 2 Timothy* the Biblical main texts were taken from a French Bible to replace Calvin's own version.

But there seems to be a serious objection to our extending this to other New Testament sermons. It is that the manuscript text for Sermons XII-XV of *I Corinthians* (and therefore presumably of *I Corinthians* as a whole) 'exactly corresponds to, for example, the 1552 Bible (Geneva, Philibert Hamelin)' as Professor Higman informs me in a letter. Of this hard fact there are only two possible explanations: Either Calvin preached on I Corinthians from this 1552 Bible; Or when the short-hand notes were turned into long-hand manuscript form, the 1552 version was substituted for Calvin's translation. Let us see if we can find out which of the two is the more probable.

All that has been said so far has been based on the assumption that Raguenier and his team of scribes pursued a uniform practice over the eleven years of his work on the sermons. But it has frequently been clear in what has been said that this was not so. For many sermons (*Jeremiah* and *Micah* among the earlier series, some *Psalms* and *I Corinthians* in the mid fifteen-fifties) only a part of the text was given, followed by 'etc.' Yet for *Isaiah* the text was given in full. And again, the text for *I Corinthians* comes from a French Bible whereas that in *Isaiah* does not.

Why there should have been this lack of consistency is not easy to decide. If the writing of the text in italic was left to the scribe, it may be that different scribes took different ways — although *Isaiah* has only the one system but many scribes. If Raguenier himself wrote all the main texts the problem becomes more puzzling. In any case, the reason why is not relevant in the textual investigation we are engaged in. The fact remains that there is inconsistency.

What is the significance of this inconsistency? Surely that we can rule out the possibility that Calvin used a French Bible when preaching. For in the case of *Isaiah* and *I Corinthians*, whereas it is credible that Raguenier (or some unknown scribe) substituted the text of a French Bible for the original text as spoken by Calvin, it is completely and utterly incredible that Raguenier (or an unknown scribe) substituted his own translation of the Hebrew text of Isaiah, complete with sensible alternative renderings, for the text of a French Bible read out by Calvin. And this same argument is valid for all the sermons.

Might it not be, however, that Calvin also was inconsistent? that, whereas Raguenier was inconsistent in not always record-

Appendix 3   177

ing the whole text, Calvin was inconsistent in not always preaching from a French Bible or one in the original tongue? In theory this is possible. If there were some years between Isaiah and I Corinthians it might even be advanced as plausible. But the two series ran concurrently, I Corinthians from October 20, 1555 until February, 1557, and Isaiah from July 16, 1556 onwards. What we should be asked to believe is that on any relevant Sunday Calvin took a 1552 French Bible into the pulpit and read his text from it and then the next day and throughout the week took a Hebrew Bible with him and translated his text extemporarily. Is it not more probable that the one whom we know from other evidence to have been inconsistent in practice, who on Sundays recorded a truncated text with 'etc.' and on weekdays wrote out Calvin's text in full, should have carried his inconsistency into sometimes giving Calvin's own text and sometimes a text from a printed Bible?

I would therefore put forward the hypothesis that Calvin took a Hebrew or Greek text into the pulpit and translated as he went along, just as he did for his lectures. The indications to the contrary arise from inconsistency in the transmission of the sermons.

Since I wrote this Appendix, Professor Higman has supplied me with some interesting additional evidence. He collated the whole of the Biblical text of 1 Timothy sermons with the Hamelin Bible mentioned above and found that there were 'five or six variants in each chapter'. But when he collated 1 Timothy with the 1544 Geneva Nouveau Testament printed by Jean Michel, they nearly always corresponded. This fits in with our earlier conclusion that for 1 Timothy the text of a French Bible was substituted for that of Calvin at either the transcription stage or for the printing.

That it was in the transcribing seems preferable in view of the variants occurring between successive repetitions of the texts, which sometimes offer a valid alternative rendering. Thus, in 1 Tim. 5.17 the 1544 N.T. reads 'Les prestres qui president' against the 1552 Bible 'Les Anciens qui president'. Sermon XLII agrees with 1544, Sermon XLIII with 1552.

The likeliest explanation is that Calvin's pulpit rendering direct from the Greek was either not recorded or, if recorded, was discarded when the transcription into long-hand was made. In either case, the text from a printed French Bible was substituted for it. That the same Bible was not used for each sermon suggests that the scribe (and not Raguenier) wrote out the initial text and that different scribes were responsible for Sermons XLII and XLIII, the one of whom possessed a 1544 N.T. and the other a 1552 Bible. On the other hand it might simply be that Raguenier wrote them out (as is generally believed) and just used any Bible that came to hand without thinking twice about it and without Calvin or anyone else paying any attention.

BIBLIOGRAPHIES

Sermons in Manuscript

In the Bibliothèque publique et universitaire de Genève.

87	sermons on 2 Samuel	ms. fr. 16
66	sermons on Isaiah 13-29	ms. fr. 17
67	sermons on Isaiah 30-41	ms. fr. 18
57	sermons on Isaiah 42-52	ms. fr. 19
25	sermons on Jeremiah 15-18	ms. fr. 20
2	sermons on Lamentations 1.1-5	ms. fr. 20
55	sermons on Ezekiel 1-15	ms. fr. 21
69	sermons on Ezekiel 23-48	ms. fr. 22
53	sermons on Ezekiel 23-35[1]	ms. fr. 23
28	sermons on Micah	ms. fr. 24
44	sermons on Acts 1-7	ms. fr. 25
58	sermons on 1 Corinthians	ms. fr. 26
24	sermons on various texts	ms. fr. 40a
7	sermons on Christ's Passion etc.	ms. fr. 40b
8	sermons presented by Raguenier	ms. fr. 40c

In other libraries.

84	sermons on Genesis	Bodleian Library, Oxford. Codex Bodl. 740
25	sermons on Genesis	Lambeth Palace Library, London, MS. 1784
2	sermons on Genesis	Bibl. Nat., Paris. Collection du Puy 268
48	sermons on Ephesians	Burgerbibliothek, Bern. Codex 193

[1] This set is a doublet of part of the preceding.

Details of ms. fr. 40 a

23 sermons by Calvin, comprising: Psalms 80.9-20; 147.12-20; 148.1-14; 149.4-9; 65.6-14; 46.7-12; 48.2-8; 48.9-15; Matthew 28.1-10 (two sermons); Acts 2.1-11.
The rest are doublets: Genesis 12.1ff.; Deuteronomy 1.1-3; Job 33.17ff.; 33.29ff.; Isaiah 33.5-10; Ezekiel 2.1-3; 2.4-5; 3.4-7; 3.10-11; 18.5; 20.30; 22.9ff.
The extra 'sermon', making the number to 24, is in fact a *Congrégation*, and not a sermon.

Details of ms. fr. 40b

Sermons on Christ's Passion: Matthew 26.40-54; 26.55-75; 26.71-27.14; 27.15-44; 27.45-56; 27.57-66.
The seventh sermon is on 2 Samuel 11.5-15.
There are besides Congrégations of 1563 and 1564.

Early French Editions

1 EXPOSI / TION SVR L'EPI - / STRE DE SAINCT IV -/ DAS APOSTRE DE NO -/ stre Seigneur Iesus Christ. / Composee par M. Iean Caluin./[Device]/1542.
A-B⁸
See p. 73

2 Deux sermons de / M. Iean Caluin, faitz en la / ville de Geneue. / L'vn le mecredy quatriesme de Nouembre / 1545. iour ordonné pour faire prieres ex- / traordinaires: apres avoir ouy nouuelles / que les Papistes auoyent esmeu guerre en / Allemaigne contre les Chrestiens./ Le second, le mecredy prochainement suy-/ uant, auquel par l'ordonnance & authori-/ té de Messieurs de la ville, on rēdit a Dieu/ action de graces solennelle, apres que nou/ uelles furent venues que Dieu auoit don-/ né victoire aux siens, & brise la force des/ ennemis./ [Device]/Imprimé à Geneue par Iean Girard./ 1546.

[Contents: two sermons on Ps. 115.1-3 and Ps. 124; also Clement Marot's verse renderings of Ps. 79 and Ps. 9 and Gueroult's verse renderings of Ps. 124 and the Te Deum. The two sermons were 'extraitz par Iean Cousin'. (sig. D5ᵛ).]
A-D⁸

3   QVATRE SERMONS / de M. Iehan Caluin, traictans des/matieres fort vtiles pour nostre/ temps, comme on pourra veoir/ par la preface./ Auec briefue exposition du Pseau-/ me LXXXVII. / [Device] / L'Oliuier de Robert Estienne./ M. D. LII.
a - i⁸, k¹⁰
[Calvin's prefatory letter is dated September 20, 1552. These are the sermons on fleeing idolatry (Ps. 16.4), enduring persecution (Heb. 13.3), the use of Church ordinances (Ps. 27.4), and the pure service of God (Ps. 27.8).]

3A SIX SERMONS DE / Ian Caluin:/ A SCAVOIR, / QVATRE EXHORTATIFS / à fuir toute idolatrie, & à endurer toutes/ persecutions, à conuerser en l'Eglise du/ Seigneur, & à librement seruir à Dieu./ ET, / DEVX, OV IL EST TRAI-/ té du seul Moyeneur de Dieu & des hōmes./ Auec brieue exposition du Pseaume,/ LXXXVII./ Par P. Iaques Poullain, & René/ Houdouyn./ M.D. LV.
A-M⁸
[A combination of Numbers 3 and 10B.]

3B *in* Recueil des opuscules, c'est à dire petits traictez de M. Iean Calvin. Genève. J.-B. Pinereul. 1566
[The Quatre sermons and Exposition sur Ps. 87.]

3C DEVX / SERMONS DE / M. IEAN CALVIN,/ L'vn, auquel tous Chrestiens sont exhortez/ de fuir l'idolatrie exterieure. Sur le troisie-/ me verset du Pseaume XVI./ L'autre, à souffrir persecution pour suiure Ie-/sus Christ & son Euangile: Sur le passage/ qui est au XIII. chap. des Hebrieux./ Pseaume 97.7/ Tous ceux qui seruent aux images soyent confus,/ & qui se glorifient és idoles./ Matth. 5.10./ Vous serez bien-heureux quand on vous aura dit/ iniure, & persecuté, & dit toute mauuaise parole/ contre vous, en mentant, à cause de moy./ M. D. LXVI. [Orleans, E. Gibier.]
A-E⁸, F⁴

3D *in* Recueil des opuscules. Genève. J. Stoer. 1611

4   VINGTDEUX/ Sermons de M. Iean/ CALVIN, AVXQVELS EST/ exposé le Pseaume cent dixneuf-/ ieme, contenāt pareil nom-/ bre de huictains./ [Device] / A GENEVE, / Par Iean Gerard./ M.D.LIIII.
A-S⁸, T⁴

[According to R. Peter, some copies, intended for distribution in France, omit the names of the author and printer and the place of printing.]

4A - A GENEVE./ M.D.LIIII. [Printer unnamed.]
a-z^8, A-O^8

4B - A GENEVE,/ PAR FRANÇOIS ESTIENNE,/ Pour Estienne Anastase./ M.D. LXII.
a-z^8, A-E^8, F^4
[Also printed for Bertrand Bodin.]

5 SERMONS DE / M. Iehan Caluin/ SVR LES DIX COMMAN-/ demens de la Loy, donnee de Dieu par/ Moyse, autrement appelez le Decalogue:/ RECVEILLIS SVR LE CHAMP ET / mot a mot de ses predications, lors qu'il preschoit le Deu-/ teronome, sãs que depuis y ait este riẽ adiousté ne diminué./ [Device]/ A GENEVE, / De l'imprimerie de Conrad Badius./ M. D. LVII.
Colophon: Achevé d'imprimer à Geneve par Conrad Badius, l'an M.D.LVII., le dernier iour d'aoust.
a-p^8

5A - Genève. C. Badius. 1558
a-z^8, A-G^8, H^4
[The sixteen sermons in Number 5, with the addition of two on Deut. 4. 15-24.]

5B - Genève. E. Anastase. 1559
a-z^8, A-G^8, H^4

5C - Genève. F. Estienne for E. le Melais. 1562.
a-z^8, A^8, B^{10}

5D - 1562. [Without place or printer, but according to R. Peter, Lyon, J. Frellon / S. Barbier.]
a-z^8, A^4

6 PLVSIEVRS SER / MONS DE IEHAN CAL-/ uin touchant la Diuinite, humanite & na-/ tiuite de nostre Seigneur Iesus Christ: Item/ touchant sa passion, mort, resurrection, ascen-/ sion, & dernier aduenement: Puis touchant la/ descente du S. Esprit sur les Apostres, & la pre/miere predication de S. Pierre:/ DESQVELS VOVS TROV-/ uerez l'ordre en la page suyuante./ [Device]/ M.D.

LVIII./ De l'imprimerie de Conrad Badius./ AVEC PRIVILEGE.
Colophon: Achevé d'imprimer à Genève par Conrad Badius l'an
M.D. LVIII, le xiiii. de iuillet.

*^{8}, **^{8}, ⚜*^{8}, a-z^8, A-V^8

[Contents: twenty-six undated sermons on (a) the subjects of Feast Days (b) Isaiah 52.13-53.12; together with a Congrégation on John 1.1-5.]

6A - Genève. Michel Blanchier. 1563.

a-z^8, A-R^8, S^4

[The same contents as Number 6, but in a different order.]

7 SERMONS DE / IEHAN CALVIN SVR LE / dixieme & onzieme chapitre de la pre-/ miere Epistre sainct Paul aux Corin-/ thiens, esquels outre plusieurs matieres/ excellentes, celle de la saincte Cene de/ nostre Seigneur Iesus Christ est fami-/ lierement declaree./ [Device]/ M.D. LVIII./De l'imprimerie de Conrad Badius./ AVEC PRIVILEGE.

a-z^8, A-L^8

7A - Genève. M. Blanchier. 1563.

a-z^8, A-K^8

8 DIXHUICT / SERMONS DE M. IEAN / CALVIN./ Ausquels, entre autres poincts, l'histoire de Melchisedec/ & la matiere de la Iustification, sont deduites, auec l'expo-/ sition de trois Cantiques, assavoir de la V. Marie, de Za-/ charie & de Simeon, nouuellement mis en lumiere./ Desquels vous trouuerez l'ordre apres la preface./ [Device]/ PAR IEAN BONNEFOY./ M. D. LX. / AVEC PRIVILEGE.

*^{8}, A-Z^8, Aa-Hh^8

[Contents: Three sermons on Melchisedech, four on Gen. 15.4-7, three on the Magnificat, one on Luke 1.56-60, five on the Benedictus, two on the Nunc dimittis.]

- A variant, Genève, Anastase, 1560.

8A TROIS / SERMONS / SVR LE SACRI-/ FICE D'ABRAHAM. / Par M. Iean Caluin./ Au commencement & à la fin du premier des-/ quels, sont inserees les Prieres que l'Auteur a ac-/ coustumees faire en les Sermons ordinaires./ [Device]/Auec Priuilege./M.D. LXI. [Without name of printer or place; but, according to R. Peter, Genève. Jacques Bourgeois.]

A-E^8, F^{10}

8B SERMONS DE / M. IEAN CALVIN. / Ausquels, entre autres poincts, l'histoire de / Melchisedec & la matiere de la iustifica-/ tion sont deduites, auec l'exposition du / sacrifice d'Abraham. / L'ordre d'iceux se trouuera en la/page suyvante./ [Device] / A GENEVE. / CHEZ IEAN DVRANT. / M. D. LXV.

a-t^8, u^4

[Contents: as Number 8, but omitting the Sermons on the Canticles and including the three in Number 8A.]

9 TRAITE / DE LA PRE-/ DESTINATION / ETERNELLE / DE DIEV. / Par laquelle les vns sont eleuz à salut, les/ autres laissez en leur condemnation. Aussi/ de la prouidence, par laquelle il gouuerne/ les choses humaines./ Item y sont adioustez treze Sermons, traitans de/ l'election gratuite de Dieu en Iacob, & de la reiection/ en Esau. Traité auquel chacun Chrestien pourra/ voir les bontez excellentes de Dieu enuers les siens,/ & ses iugemens merueilleux enuers les reprouuez./ Nouuellement exposez par M./ Iean Caluin. / ❦ / PAR Antoine Cercia, / L'AN M. D. LX.

a-z^8, A-Q^8

- A variant: Genève. Iean Durand. 1560.

9A TREZE / SERMONS / DE M. I. CALVIN, / Traitans de l'election . . . enuers les reprouuez. [As Number 9] / Recueillis de ses predications/ l'an mil cinq cens soixante./ Rom.11.33./ O profondes richesses de la sapience &/ cognoissance de Dieu, que ses iugemēs sont/ incomprehensibles, & ses voyes impossibles à trouuer!/ M.D. LXII. [Without place or printer, but according to R. Peter, Genève, J. Crespin.]

A-T^8

10 SERMONS DE / Iean Caluin sur les deux E-/ pistres S. Paul a Timothee,/ & sur l'Epistre a Tite./ [Device] / IMPRIME/ A Geneue par Conrad Badius,/ M. D. LXI.
Colophon: Achevé d'imprimer par Conrad Badius l'an M. D. LXI, le vingtieme iour de fevrier.

*^{4}, a-z^6, A-Y^6, Z^4

10A - Genève. Jean Bonnefoy. 1563.

*^{4}, a-z^4, A-Z^4, Aa-Zz^4, AAa-HHh^4, IIi^6

10B DEVX SER-/ MONS DE M./ Iean Caluin prins de la premiere/ Epistre à Timothée au second/ Chapitre sur ces parolles. Car il y a/ vn seul Moyenneur de Dieu, & des/hōmes, assauoir Iesus Christ,

&c./ Ou il est traité d'vn seul Moyenneur, de Dieu/ & des hommes./ [Device]/ De l'Imprimerie de Iean Gerard./ 1555.
$$a\text{-}e^8$$
[In the photocopy I have seen of this title page, the date is blotted out by the library stamp - Bayerische. I supply 1555 on the authority of R. Peter.]

10C The Deux Sermons are included in the Six Sermons, Number 3A.

10D SERMON / DE M. I. CAL. OV IL / EST MONTRE QVELLE / doit estre la modestie des/ Femmes en leurs ha-/ billements./ I. IEAN. 2. Tout ce qui est au monde (assauoir, la conuoitise de/ la chair, & conuoitise des yeux, & outrecuydance de/ la vie) n'est point du pere, mais du monde. Et le mon/ de passe & sa conuoitise: mais qui faict la volonté de/ Dieu, demeure eternellement./ 1561. [Without place or printer.]
$$A\text{-}B^8, C^4$$
[This is Sermon XVII from the 1 Timothy series.]

11 SERMONS / DE IEHAN CALVIN / Sur le Cantique que feit le bon Roy/ Ezechias apres qu'il eut este malade/ & affligé de la main de Dieu, selon/ qu'il est contenu en Isaie, chapitre/ XXXVIII./ [Device]/ A Geneve,/ Par François Estienne,/ Pour Bertrand Bodin./ M. D. LXII.
$$a\text{-}e^8, f^2, g^8$$
[Four sermons, taken from the 1556-1559 series on Isaiah. R. Peter records four variants, with Bodin, Anastase, Bres, and Robinet respectively collaborating with Estienne.]

12 SOIXANTE CINQ/ Sermons de Iean Cal-/ VIN SVR L'HARMONIE / OV CONCORDANCE DES TROIS / Euāgelistes, S. Matthieu, sainct/ Marc, & S. Luc./ RECVEILLIS FIDELE-/ mēt par feu M. Denys Ragueneau, à mesure/ qu'on les preschoit./ [Device]/ A GENEVE./ Imprimé par Conrad Badius,/ M. D. LXII.
Colophon: Achevé d'imprimer par Conrad Badius, l'an M. D. LXII, le XIX iour du mois de ianvier.
$$*^6, a\text{-}z^8, A\text{-}Z^8, AA\text{-}ZZ^8, AAa\text{-}DDd^8, EEe^4$$

12A - Lyon. 1562 [No printer's name but J. Frellon and S. Barbier, according to R. Peter.]
$$*^8, a\text{-}z^8, A\text{-}Z^8, aa\text{-}yy^8$$

12B - Genève. Jacob Stoer. 1590.

*⁴,***⁴, ****⁴, *****⁶, a-z⁶, A-Z⁶, AA-RR⁶, SS⁴

13 SERMONS DE / IEAN CALVIN SVR/L'EPISTRE S. PAVL APOSTRE/ aux Ephesiens./ [Device] / A GENEVE, / DE L'IMPRIMERIE / De Iean Baptiste Pinereul. / M. D. LXII.
)(⁴, a-z⁸, A–Z⁸, Aa-Nn⁸, Oo⁴

13A - [Without place or printer, but according to R. Peter Lyon. J. Frellon and S. Barbier.] 1562.
*⁴, a-z⁸, A-Z⁸, Aa-Ee⁸

14 SERMONS / DE M. IEAN / Caluin sur le liure/ de/ IOB./ Recueillis fidelement de sa bouche selon/ qu'il les preschoit./ A GENEVE. / M. D. LXIII.
Colophon: Achevé d'imprimer par Iean de Laon, l'an M. D. LXIII, le premier iour de iuin.
*⁴, A-Z⁴, Aa-Zz⁴, Aaa-Zzz⁴, Aaaa-Zzzz⁴, Aaaaa-Ttttt⁴, Vvvvv⁶

14A - Genève. F. Perrin. 1569.
⁴, *⁴, **⁴, ***⁴, ****⁴, a-z⁶, A-Z⁶, Aa-Yy⁶, Zz⁴

14B - Genève. Matthieu Berjon. 1611.
⁴, *⁴, **⁴, ***⁴, ****⁴, a-z⁶, A-Z⁶, Aa-Yy⁶, Zz⁴
Variant: Genève, pour Jean Vignon. 1611.

15 SERMONS DE/ IEAN CALVIN / SVR L'EPISTRE S. / Paul Apostre aux/ Galates. / [Device] / A GENEVE, / DE L'IMPRIMERIE DE / FRANCOIS PERRIN. / M. D. LXIII.
Colophon: Achevé d'imprimer le premier iour du mois de fevrier M. D. LXIII.
*⁴, a-z⁸, A-Z⁸, Aa-Ff⁸, Gg⁴

16 QVARANTE SEPT / SERMONS DE M. IEAN / CALVIN SVR LES HVICT / DERNIERS CHAPITRES / DES PROPHETIES / DE DANIEL./ Recueillis fidelement de sa bouche selon/ qu'il les preschoit./ [Device] / A LA ROCHELLE./ De l'Imprimerie de Barthelemi Berton. / M.D. LXV.
*⁶, A-X⁶, Y⁸
[A pirated edition, copied from the Raguenier MSS.]

Variant: - La Rochelle. Berton. Pour Pierre Chefdorge. 1565.

17 SERMONS / DE M. IEAN CAL-/ uin sur le v. liure de Moyse/

nommé Deuteronome./ RECVEILLIS FIDELEMENT DE MOT / à mot, selon qu'il les preschoit publiquement./ Auec une preface des Ministres de l'Eglise de Geneue, & un aduertisse-/ ment fait par les Diacres. / Il y a aussi deux tables: l'une des matieres principales, l'autre des passages de la Bible alle-/ guez par l'autheur en ces Sermons./ [Device]/ A GENEVE. / De l'imprimerie de Thomas Courteau. M. D. LXVII.

*[6], a-b[8], c-z[6], aa-zz[6], aaa-zzz[6], aaaa-zzzz[6], aaaaa-fffff[6], ggggg[2], hhhhh[6], iiiii[4]

Latin Translations

18   IOANNIS CALVINI / HOMILIAE QVA -/ tuor, grauem atque his temporibus admodum/ opportunam & vtilem admonitionem atque/ exhortationem continentes, quemadmodum/ ex ipsa praefatione perspici poterit./ Breuis item explanatio Psalmi LXXXVII./ ab eodem authore latinè scripta./ E GALLICO IPSIVS AVTHORIS SER-/mone in latinū à Claudio Baduello cōuersae./ GENEVAE./ EX OFFICINA IOANNIS CRISPINI./ 1553.

A-N[8]

[Translation of Number 3.]

18A   IOANNIS / CALVINI HOMI-/ LIAE SIVE CON-/ CIONES / VII./ Harū concionū argumēta, & ipsam versio-/ nis rationē Praefationes cōmonstrabūt./ [Device] / EX OFFICINA TYPOGRAPHICA / IOANNIS CRISPINI. / M. D. LVI.

A-N[8], a-f[8]

[Contents: The Quatuor Homiliae together with the first three sermons on Ps. 119 translated into Latin.]

After this the Quatuor Homiliae were not printed separately but included in the collected treatises:

18B   *in* Tractatus theologici omnes. Geneva. P de Saint-Andre. 1576.
   - Reprinted 1597.
   A new edition, by Commelin, Heidelberg, 1611.
   Two new editions by J. Stoer, Geneva, 1611 and 1612.

19   IOHANNIS / CALVINI / IN LIBRVM IOBI / CONCIONES. / Ab ipsius Concionantis ore fideliter exceptae, ac saepius antea/ Gallice, nunc vero primum Latine editae./ Adiecto duplici Indice: vno locorum Scripturae, qui hic/ citantur atque explicantur: altero praecipuorum/ doctrinae capitum, rerumque/ magis insignium./

Cum Praefatione THEODORI BEZAE./ [Device] / GENEVAE,/ APVD HAEREDES EVSTATHII VIGNON./ M. D. XCIII.

*⁴, **⁴, ***⁴, ****⁶, a-z⁶, A-Z⁶, AA-RR⁶, SS⁴

20   IOANNIS / CALVINI / HOMILIAE IN / I. LIBRVM SA-/ MVELIS./ EX GALLICIS LATINAE FACTAE / & nunc primum in lucem editae. / [Device] / GENEVAE / EXCVDEBAT GABRIEL CARTERIVS. / M. DCIIII.

)(², A-Z⁶, Aa-Zz⁶, Aaa-Ccc⁶, Ddd-Eee⁴, *⁸

English Translations

21   Certaine homi=/ lies of .m. Ioan Calvi/ ne´conteining profitable and/ necessarie´ admonitiō for this time / with an Apologie of/ Robert Horn./ Imprĩted at Rome´ before the castle of .s.Angel/ at the signe of .s.Peter. Anno./ M. D. Liii.

A-G⁸, H⁴

[Contents: The first two sermons of Number 3; translated from Number 18.]

21A   FOVRE GOD-/ lye sermons agaynst/ THE POLLVTION OF IDOLA-/ tries, comforting men in persecuti=/ ons, and teachyng them what com/ modities thei shal find in Christes/ church, which were preached in/ French by the moste famous/ Clarke Ihon Caluyne, and / translated fyrst into La=/ tine and afterward into/ Englishe by diuers/ godly learned/ men./ PSAL. 16./ I wyl not take the name of the Idols/ in my mouth./ ¶ Printed at London by Rouland Hall,/ dwelling in Golding lane at the signe/ of the thre arrowes./ 1561.

A-N⁸, O⁴

21B   Foure/ SERMONS OF / Maister Iohn Caluin,/ Entreating of matters very/ profitable for our time, as may/ bee seene by the Pre=/ face:/ With a briefe exposition of the/ LXXXVII. Psalme./ Translated out of Frenche into/ Englishe by Iohn Fielde./ Imprinted at London/ for Thomas Man, dwelling/ in Pater Noster Rowe, at the/ Signe of the Talbot./ 1579.

Colophon: Imprinted at London, at the three cranes, in the Vinetree, by Thomas Dawson, for Thomas Man. 1579.

⁴, ❊², A-G⁸, H⁴

[This, as Field says in his dedication to the Earl of Huntington, is the first translation from the French of these sermons: 'I especially following maister Caluine's french copie, somewhat differing from

21C A Sermon of/ the famous and/ Godly learned man, ma-/ ster Iohn Caluine, chiefe/ Minister and Pastour of Christs/ church at Geneua, conteining/ an exhortation to suffer perse-/ cution for followinge Iesus/ Christe and his Gospell, vp-/ pon this Text fol-/ lowing./ Heb. 13.13/ Go ye out of the Tents af-/ ter Christe, bearing his/ rebuke./ Translated out of French into/ english,/ Imprinted at London by Ro-/bert VValdegraue for/ Edward VVhite./ 1581.
A-B^8, C^6
[This is a borrowing by one 'I.P.' of Field's translation.]

21D Two godly and learned/ Sermons, made by that fa-/ mous and woorthy instrument in/ Gods church, M. Iohn Caluin. Which/ Sermons were long since translated out of/ Latine into English, by M. Robert Horne/ late Byshop of Winchester, at what time/ he suffered exile from his Country, for the te-/ stimony of a good conscience, as his A-/ pology in the beginning of the/ booke will witnes./ And because these Sermons haue/ long lyen hidden in silence, and many/ godly and religious persons, haue beene/ very desirous of them: at theyr ear-/ nest request they are nowe/ published by/ A.M./ At London/ Printed for Henry Car,/ and are to be sold in Paules Churchyard,/ ouer against the signe of the/ blasing Starre. [1584]
A^4, B-K^8
[A.M. is Anthony Munday, as the signature to the dedication shows. The date of 1584 is given on the verso of the title-page.]

22 SERMONS/ OF JOHN CAL-/ VIN, VPON THE SONGE/ that Ezechias made af-/ ter he had been sicke, and/ afflicted by the hand of/ God,/ conteyned in the 38. Chapi=/ ter of Esay./ ¶ Translated out of Frenche/ into Englishe,/ 1560./ ☞ Newly set fourth and allowed, accordyng to/ the order appointed in the Quenes Ma=/ iesties Iniunctions./ ¶ Imprinted at London, ouer Aldersgate,/ by Iohn Day./ And are there to be solde at his shoppe/ under the Gate./ ¶ Cum Gratia & priuilegio/ Regiae maiestatis.
A-G^8, Aa^8
[The translator, we learn from the signature to the dedication, was A.L. An inscription in the British Library copy reads: 'Liber Henrici Lock ex dono Annae uxoris suae. 1559.' It is to be inferred, therefore, that A.L. was Anne Lock. She was one of the Marian refugees in Geneva and, we may assume, was present when the sermons were preached on November 5, 6, 15, and 16, 1557. As no

Calvin's Preaching

edition of a French original is known, it seems that she acquired a manuscript copy of Raguenier's MSS.]

22A Foure sermons of Iohn Calvin, upon the song that king Ezechias made after hee had been sicke... conteyned in the 38. chapiter of the prophet Esay. London. John Day. 1574.
[The only known copy (in the British Museum Library) was destroyed in the 1939-45 war.]

23 THRE NOTA=/ Ble sermones, made by the godly and famous/ Clerke Maister Iohn Caluyn, on/ thre seuerall Sondayes in Maye, the yere/ 1561. upon the Psalm. 46. Teaching us con=/ stantly to cleaue unto Gods truth in time/ of aduersitie and trouble, and neuer to/ shrinke for any rage of the wicked, but/ to suffer all thynges in fayth and/ hope in Iesus Christ.Englished/ by William Warde. / [Device]/ PRINTED AT LON/ don by Rouland Hall, dwellynge in/ Gutter Lane, at the sygne of the/ halfe Egle and the Keye./ 1562.
A-F^8
[Contents: Sermons on (1) Ps. 46.1-6 (May 12, 1560 - not 1561 as the title), (2) Ps. 46.7-12 (May 19, 1560), and (3) Ps. 48.1-7 (May 26, 1560) - not Ps. 46 as the title. For an account of these sermons, which are extant only in this English translation, see R. Stauffer: Eine Englische Sammlung von Calvinpredigten.]

24 SERMONS /of Master Iohn/ Caluin, vpon the/ Booke of/ IOB./ *Translated out of French/ by Arthur Golding./ IMPRINTED / BY LVCAS HARISON AND / GEORGE / BYSHOP.
Colophon: IMPRINTED AT LONDON BY/ Henrie Binneman, for Lucas Harison/ and George Bishop. Anno 1574.
a^4, *^{6}, **^{8}, A-Y^8, Aa-Yy^8, Aaa-Ccc^8
[The dedication to the Earl of Leicester is dated December 31, 1573. In it Golding says that 'this woork is the first of any greate weyght that euer I translated out of the French toong to be published' (sig. a iij^v).]

24A A second impression was issued in the same year by the same printer and booksellers. The pagination and signatures differ, however, and an Index of Scripture is added.
a^4, -^{4}, *-****^{4}, A-Z^8, Aa-Zz^8, Aaa-Ddd^8, Eee-Fff^6

24B - IMPRINTED/ at London for George/ Byshop and Thomas/ Woodcocke./ 1579.

Colophon: Imprinted at the three cranes in the vintre by Thomas Dawson for George Bishop and Thomas Woodcocke. Anno 1580.
A⁴, *⁶, ** ⁸, A-Y⁸, Aa-Yy⁸, Aaa-Ccc⁸

24C - LONDINI/ Impensis Thomae/ Woodcocke./ 1584.
Colophon: Imprinted in London at the three cranes in the vintree by Thomas Dawson for George Byshop and Thomas Woodcocke. Anno 1584.
A⁴, ⁶ ⁸, A-Y⁸, Aa-Yy⁸, Aaa-Ccc⁸

25 SERMONS / of M. Iohn Cal-/ uine vpon the Epistle/ of Saincte Paule/ to the Gala-/ thians./ ¶ Imprinted at Lon-/ don, by Lucas Harison and/ George Bishop./ 1574.
Colophon: Imprinted at London by Henrie Bynneman for Lucas Haryson and George Byshop.
⁴, ≠⁴, *⁴, **⁴, ***⁴, A-Z⁸, Aa-Ss⁸, Tt²
[The dedication (to 'Sir William Cecill knight, baron of Burleigh') is dated 'Written at my lodging in the forestreete without Cripplegate, the 14. of november 1574' and signed 'Arthur Golding'.]

26 THE / SERMONS / of M. Iohn Caluin,/ vpon the Epistle of S./ Paule too the Ephe-/ sians./ Translated out of French into/ English by Arthur/ Golding./ ☞ Imprinted at London/ for Lucas Harison, and/ George Byshop./ 1577.
*⁸, ⁸, A-Y⁸, Aa-Xx⁸, Yy⁴
[The dedication (to Archbishop Grindal) is dated 'Written at Clare in Suffolke, the vii. of january 1576'. A replica has been published by Banner of Truth Press.]

27 Thirteene/ SERMONS OF / Maister Iohn Caluine,/ Entreating of the Free Election/ of God in Iacob, and of re-/probation in Esau./ A treatise wherin euery Christian/ may see the excellent benefites of God to-/ wardes his children, and his maruelous/ iudgements towards the reprobate, firste/ published in the French toung, & now/ Translated into Englishe by/ Iohn Fielde, For the/ comfort of all/ Christians./ Rom. 11.33./ O the deepenes of the riches, both of the vvisdome and/ knowledge of God! Howe vnsearchable are his/ iudgements, and his vvayes past finding out./ Imprinted at London for Thomas/ Man and Tobie Cooke./ 1579.
Colophon: Imprinted at London by Thomas Dawson, dwelling at the three cranes in the vinetree, for Tobie Cooke and Thomas Man. 1579.
[The dedication is dated October 25, 1579.]

A-B⁴, B-Z⁸

28 ¶ SERMONS / of M. Iohn Caluine,/ vpon the .X. Commande-/ mentes of the Lawe, geuen of/ God by Moses, otherwise/ called the Decalogue./ Gathered word for word, pre/sently at his Sermons, when he/ preached on Deuteronomie, without/ adding vnto, or diminishing/ from them any thing af-/ terward./ Translated out of Frenche/ into English, by I. H./ ¶ Imprinted at Lon-/ don, for Iohn Hari-/ son, 1579.

Colophon: Imprinted at London at the three cranes of the vinetree by Thomas Dawson for Iohn Harison. 1579.

[I.H. was, as the dedication shows, John Harmar or Harmer. He was Professor of Greek at Oxford and translated also some Chrysostom and Beza. Two other booksellers besides Harison were involved - George Bishop and Thomas Woodcocke.]

*⁴, A-Z⁴, Aa-Hh⁴, Ii²

28A - Imprinted at London/ for George Bishop./ 1581.
[The printer was T. Dawson. Variants were 'for Iohn Harison' and 'for Thomas Woodcocke'.]

29 SERMONS/ of M. Iohn Caluin,/ on the Epistles of S. Paule/ to Timothie and/ Titus./ Translated out of French/ into English, by/ L.T./ AT LONDON/ Imprinted for G. Bishop/ and T. Woodcoke./ 1579.

⁸, A-Z⁸, Aa-Zz⁸, Aaa-Zzz⁸, Aaaa-Iiii⁸

[L.T. was Laurence Tomson.]

29A TVVO/ GODLY AND NO=/ TABLE SERMONS/ PREACHED/ BY THE / excellent and famous Clarke,/ master Iohn Caluyne, in the yere. 1555. The one concer=/ nynge Pacience in aduersitie:/ The other touchyng the/ most comfortable as=/ surance of oure/ saluation in/ Chryste. /Iesu./ Translated out of Frenche/ into Englyshe.

Colophon: Imprynted at London by Wyllyam Seres, dwelling at the west ende of Paules churche at the sygne of the hedgehogge. Cum priuilegio ad imprimendum solum.

A-F⁸, G⁴

[Contents: Sermon IV of the series on 2 Timothy (2 Tim. 1.8-9) preached on 'Sondaye the v. of may 1555, in the forenone', and Sermon V (2 Tim. 1.8b-10) preached on 'Sonday the v. of maye 1555, after dyner'. The fact that precise dates are given shows that the translation was not made from Number 10, which has no dates, but from a transcription of the MSS. Translator unknown.]

30 Two and twentie/ Sermons of Maister/ Iohn Caluin./ In which Sermons is most religi-/ ously handled, the hundredth and nine-/ teenth Psalme of Dauid, by eight/ verses aparte according to/ the Hebrewe Al-/ phabet./ Translated out of French into/ Englishe by T.S./ ¶ Imprinted at London/for Iohn Harison and/ Thomas Man,/ 1580.
Colophon: Imprinted at London at the three cranes in the vintree by Thomas Dawson for Iohn Harison and Thomas Man. 1580.
$4, A-Z^8, Aa^6$
[Date and signature of dedication: 'From Mildenhall, the 4. of november 1579. Your worships to command in the Lorde. Tho. Stocker.']

31 Diuers Sermons of Ma-/ ster Iohn Caluin, concerning the/ Diuinitie, Humanitie, and Natiui-/ tie of our Lorde Iesus Christe:/ As also touching his Passion, Death,/ Resurrection, Ascention: togeather/ with the comming downe of the holy/ Ghoste vpon his Apostles: and the/ first Sermon of S. Peter./ The order of which you shall finde in/ the Page ensuing./ ¶ At London printed/ for George Byshop./ 1581.
Colophon: Imprinted at London by Thomas Dawson for George Bishop. 1581.
$*^4, **^2, A^4, B-Z^8, Aa-Cc^8$
[Dedication dated 'London, the vi. of may 1581. Thomas Stocker.' This is a translation of the second edition (1563) of Plusieurs sermons, Number 6A.]

32 THE / SERMONS / OF M. IOHN CALVIN / VPON THE FIFTH BOOKE OF/ Moses called Deuteronomie:/ Faithfully gathered word for word as he preached/ them in open Pulpet;/ Together with a preface of the Ministers of the Church of/ Geneua, and an admonishment made by the Deacons there./ Also there are annexed two profitable Tables, the one containing/ the chiefe matters; the other the places of Scripture herein alledged./ Translated out of French by ARTHVR GOLDING./ [Device] / AT LONDON,/ Printed by Henry Middleton/ for THOMAS WOODCOCKE./ Anno Domini 1583.
$6, A-Z^6, Aa-Zz^6, Aaa-Zzz^6, Aaaa-Zaaa^6, Aaaaa-Yyyyy^6, Zzzzz^4, *^8$
Two variants: (1) for George Bishop, (2) for John Harison.
[Dedication dated 'the xxj. of december 1582. At the end of the last sermon is the following notice: Heere ende the Sermons which were

made vpon the fifth booke of Moses/ called Deuteronomie by M. Iohn Caluin minister of Gods/ word in the Church of Geneue, and were gathered/ by Dyonis Raguenier, borne in Bar, stan-/ding vpon the riuer Seine./ Translated out of French into English by Arthur Golding.]

33 SERMONS / of Maister Iohn Caluin,/ on the Historie of Melchi-/sedech: Wherein is also handled,/ Abrahams courage in rescuing his Nephew/ Lot: and his Godlines in paying tithes/ to Melchisedech./ Also,/ Abrahams Faith, in belieuing God: com-/prehending foure Sermons./ And,/ Abrahams Obedience, in offering his/ sonne Isaack; in three Sermons./ Translated out of French, by Thomas/ Stocker, Gent./ LONDON/ Printed by Iohn Windet, and are/ to be sold at the shop of Andrew Maunsell,/ in the Royall Exchaunge./ 1592.

A^4, B-M^8, N^6, O-X^8

German Translations

34 Vier Predigten H. Iohann Caluini / Deren drey uber den/ Englischen Gruss handlen von Gott=/ licher Verheissung und/ Allmacht:/ Die vierdte aber uber das funffte Ge=/ bott vom schuldigen gehorsam gegen/ allen Oberherrn. Aus dem Frantzosischen trewlich verteutscht./ [Device]/ Gedruckt zu Herborn in der Graffschafft/ Nassaw Catzenelnbogen &. durch/ Christoff Raben./ M.D. LXXXVI.

):(^{2}, a-i^4, k^2

[Contents: Three sermons on the Annunciation (Luke 1.26-38) taken from the series on the Harmonie des trois Euangelistes, and Sermon XXXVI from the series on Deuteronomy, on the Fifth Commandment, Deut. 5.16.]

35 Predigten/ H. IOHAN-/ NIS CALVINI / uber das buch Iob:/ Wie dieselbe auss seinem mund durch be=/ felch eines ehrsamen Rahts zu Genff seind/ verzeichnet worden./ Der este Theil./ Auss dem Frantzosischen trewlich verteutscht./ [Device]/ Gedruckt zu Herborn in der Graffschafft Nassaw / Catzenelnbogen &. durch Christof Raben. / M.D. LXXXVII. 4 Bände

Colophon: Getruckt zu Herborn, in der Graffschafft Nassaw, Catzenelnbogen, &.. durch Christof Raben. M. D. LXXXVII.

Bänd 1:):(^{4}, A-Z^8, Aa-Nn^8, Oo^6

Band 2: a-z^8, aa-rr^8, ss^{10}

Band 3: aaa-zzz^8, Aaa-Ttt^8, Vvv^6
Band 4: AA-ZZ^8, AAA-SSS^8, TTT^{10}

35A PRECES ET SOLILOQUIA:/ Christliche˙ ausserlesene/ Gebett˙ und heimliche gesprech/ beyde mit Gott und mit ihm selbst˙ in/ allerley not unnd anligen˙ so einem wahren/ Christen' beydes an leib unnd seele˙ in der/ Pilgramschafft dieses lebens widerfa=/ ren mögen./ Mehrertheils auss den herrlichen Pre=/ digten des fürnemsten Euangelischen Leh-/ rers in Franckreich˙ uber das Buch Iob˙/ zusammen gebracht./ Sampt vielen andern sehr Gottseligen unnd/ eiferigen Gebetten˙ welcher sich zu diesen letzten/ zeiten viel heiliger Märtyrer in Franckreich˙ Engelland˙ Ni=/ derland und anderswo in ihren höchsten nöten gebraucht ha=/ ben: newlich auss dem Frantzösischen Märtyrbuch/ von einem trewhertzigen Christen/ verteuschet./ 2. Timoth. 2.v.22./ Iage nach der gerechtigkeit˙ dem glauben˙ der lieb˙ dem/ fride˙ mit allen˙ die den Herrn anruffen von reinem/ hertzen./ Gedruckt zu Herborn in der Graffschafft/ Nassaw˙ Catzenelnbogen˙ &. durch/ Christoff Raben./ M. D. XCII.
Colophon: Gedruckt zu Herborn in der Graffschafft Nassaw, &. durch Christoff Raben. M. D. XCII.
)(^{12}, A-P^{12}
[Prayers taken from the German translation of the series on Job, with prayers of martyrs from Crespin's *Le livre des Martyrs*.]

36 Der 119. Psalm/ Des Königes/ und Propheten Da=/ vids./ Erkläret und Aussgelegt in/ Zwo und zwantzig Predigten/ Durch/ Herrn Johan Calvin,/ weyland Dienern des Wortts Gottes / in der Kirchen zu Genff./ Jetzt allererst auss der Frantzösischen/ Sprach˙ in die Teutsche übergesetzt./ 1. Thess. 5./ 20. Die Weissagungen verachtet nicht./ 21. Prüfet alles˙ das gute behaltet Meidet allen schet- [letters illegible] des bösen./ Gedruckt zu Cassel˙ durch Wilhelm/ Wessel' Anno 1615.
A^8, B^8, B^8, C-X^8, Z^8, Aa-Zz^8 Aaa-Qqq^8, Rrr^2

Dutch Translations

37 Predicatien/ Iohannis Caluini/ ouer den Lofsanck des/ Coninckx Ezechie die hy dede/ na dat hy cranck˙ eñ vande handt/ Godts was gheslaghen gheweest˙ / ghelyck dien is beschreuen byden/ Prophete Esaias aen het/ achtendertichste/ Capittel:/ Nv eerst ghetrouwelijck vvter/ Fransoyscher talen in Ne=/ derduytsche ouer=/ ghesedt

door/ Th. O./ THANTVVERPEN./ By Iasper Troyen, vvoonende op/ de Catte-veste inden ten-/ nen Pot./ Anno 1581.
A-H⁸

38 Vergaderinghe ofte proef-predicke, gedaen, op het beginsel van den Evangelio des heyligen Ioannis:... Mitsgaders: een predicatie vander geboorten onses Heeren Iesu Christi,... Item, noch neghen predicatien,... over-gheset uyt den franchoysche tale, in onse neder duytsche sprake, door Ian Martini. Tot Delf ghedruckt by Ian Andriesz., 1598.
Ff. 140. A-S⁸
[Contents: *Congrégation* on John 1.1-5; Sermon on Luke 2.1-14; and nine Sermons on Matt. 26-28. I am very grateful to Dr. J.-F. Gilmont for sending me the bibliographical information. R. Peter knew of this book only from a nineteenth century edition (Dordrecht. J.P. Revers. 1855). Dr. Gilmont has discovered a copy in the University of Gand.]

39 XL./ Predicatien Ioannis Cal=/ vini´ ghetogen uyt alle zyne Sermonen die/ hy ghedaen heeft over het Boeck Iob./ Seer dienstich voor benaude, cleynmoedighe, verslaghene/ ende aenghevochtene herten./ Tot troost´ onderwysinghe ende verstserckinghe der selver:/ UYt de/ Franscoysche in onse Nederlandtsche/ Tale over-gheset./ Door VV. S./[Device] / Iob 14,1./ De mensche van eener vrouwen gheboren, leeft eenen corten/ tijdt, ende is vol onrusten./ Ghedruckt t'Amstelredam voor Laurens/ Iacobsz. op't Water inden vergulden Bybel./ Anno 1602.
A⁴, B², C-Z⁸, Aa-Tt⁸
[Translator's preface dated from Amsterdam, July 7, 1602. Contents: forty of the 159 Sermons on Job. The selection is of the passages containing Job's own words.]

40 Thien/ Predicatien´/ IOANNIS CALVINI,/ In welcke onder andere de gheschie=/ denisse Melchisedechs´ ende den handel/ der rechtveerdighmakinghe´ met/ de verclaringhe van Abra=/ hams offerhande ver=/ haelt worden./ Welcker inhoudt men vinden sal op/ d'anderzyde deses Bladts./ Eerst inde Fransche Tale ghedruckt/ tot Geneve, by Ian Durant: Ende nu in onse/ Nederduytsche sprake ghetrouwelijck/ verduyscht door I. MARTINI./ TOT DELF./ Ghedruckt by Ian Andriess./ Boeck-vercooper aen't Marct-/ veldt´ in't Gulden A B C./ ANNO M. CCCCCC. IIII.
[Contents: the three sermons on Melchisedech, the four on justifi-

cation, and the three on Abraham's sacrifice.]

Sermons in Supplementa Calviniana

SC I.	2 Samuel (87)	[ms. fr. 16]
SC II.	Isaiah 13-29 (66)	[ms. fr. 17]
SC III.	Isaiah 30-41 (67)	[ms. fr. 18]
SC IV	Isaiah 42-52 (57)	[ms. fr. 19]
SC V	Micah (28)	[ms. fr. 24]
SC VI	Jeremiah 14. 19-18.23 (25) Lamentations 1.1-5 (2)	[ms. fr. 20]
SC VII	Psalms etc.	[ms. fr. 40a and 40b; & Paris]
SC VIII	Genesis (?)	[Bodleian, Lambeth, Paris]
SC IX	Ezekiel (?)	[ms. fr. 21, 22, 23, 40a]
SC X	Ezekiel (?)	[ms. fr. 21, 22, 23, 40a]

SC VII contains also one of three sermons in Psalm 46 which is extant only in an English translation. Although the book had been mentioned in a bibliography of 1852, it had dropped out of notice until I included it in the Bibliography of my book *The Oracles of God*. Since then Richard Stauffer has written a bibliographical piece on it, which is reprinted in SC VII. pp. 12-14.

Sermons in Corpus Reformatorum

The number of sermons is given in brackets.

Genesis
    Melchizedek [3]   CO 23. 625-740
    Abraham's sacrifice [3]   CO 23. 741-784
    Jacob and Esau [13]   CO 58. 1-198

Deuteronomy [200]   CO 25. 605- 29.232

1 Samuel (Latin) [107]   CO 29. 241 - 30.734

Psalms [24]
    Psalm 115 [1]   CO 32. 455-466
    Psalm 124 [1]   CO 32. 467-480
    Psalm 119 [22]   CO 32. 481-752

Job [159]   CO 33. 21- 35.514

Isaiah [11]
    Hezekiah (Isa. 38) [4]   CO 35.517-580
    Isa. 52.12 - 53 [7]   CO 35. 581-688

Daniel [47]   CO 41. 323- 42. 174

Harmony of Gospels [65]   CO 46. 1-826
    Matthew 26-28 [9]   CO 46. 829-954
    Luke 2. 1-14 [1]   CO 46. 955-968
    John 1.1-5 [1]   CO 47. 461-484

Acts
    1.1-11 [4]   CO 48.577-622
    2.1-4, 13-24 [5][1]   CO 48.623-664

1 Corinthians 10-11 [19]   CO 49.577-830

Galatians [43]   CO 50.273- 51.136

Ephesians [48]   CO 51.241-862

2 Thessalonians 1.6-10[1]   CO 52. 219-238

1 Timothy [54]   CO 53. 1-658

2 Timothy [30]   CO 54. 1-370

Titus [17]   CO 54.373-596

Matieres fort utiles [4]   CO 8.369-452

---

[1] In fact, only 4 sermons. Number 2 is omitted.

Bibliographies

Works by Calvin

Ioannis Calvini Opera quae supersunt omnia. Ediderunt G. Baum, E. Cunitz, E. Reuss. 59 volumes (Corpus Reformatorum.) Brunswick and Berlin, 1863-1900 (see pp. 197-198 for details).

Joannis Calvini Opera Selecta. Ediderunt P. Barth, W. Niesel, D. Scheuner. 5 volumes. München, 1926-52.

Supplementa Calviniana. Sermons Inédits. Neukirchen, (1936) 1961ff. (see p. 197 for details).

Institution de la Religion Chrestienne. Edited by J.-D. Benoît. 4 volumes. Paris, 1957-63.

Sermons on Isaiah's Prophecy of the Death and Passion of Christ. Translated and edited by T.H.L. Parker. London, 1956.

Other Works Mentioned

Andrewes, Lancelot: Ninety-Six Sermons. 5 volumes. Oxford, 1841-43.
Bright, T.: Characterie: an Arte of Shorte, Swifte, and Secrete Writing by Character. London, 1588.
Bullinger, H.: The Decades. Translated by H.I. Edited for the Parker Society by T. Harding. Cambridge, 1849-52.
Brooks, Phillips: Lectures on Preaching. (Lyman Beecher Lectures, Yale, 1877). London, n.d.
Cassell's French-English, English-French Dictionary. London, 1973.
Colladon, N.: Vie de Calvin (CO 21).
Crespin, J.: Le Livre des Martyrs. Genève, 1554ff.
Dodd, C.H.: The Apostolic Preaching and its Developments. London, 1936.
Doumergue, E.: Jean Calvin. Les hommes et les choses de son temps. 7 volumes. Paris, 1899-1927.
Forsyth, P.T.: Positive Preaching and the Modern Mind (Lyman Beecher Lectures, Yale, 1907). London, 1909.
Gagnebin, B.: L'Histoire des Manuscrits des Sermons de Calvin. (SC II, pp. XIVff.).
Hooker, Richard: The Works of... Arranged by the Rev. John Keble. 3 volumes. Oxford, 1845.

Littré É.: Dictionnaire de la Langue Française. 4 volumes. Paris, 1873.
Miles, D.M.: Calvin's New Testament Sermons: A homiletical Survey. Dissertation in Cambridge University Library.
Mülhaupt, E.: Die Predigt Calvins, ihre Geschichte, ihre Form und ihre religiösen Grundgedanken. Berlin, 1931
Newman, J.H.,: Parochial and Plain Sermons. 8 volumes. Oxford, 1868/69.
Original Letters Relative to the English Reformation. Edited by H. Robinson. 2 volumes. Cambridge, 1846-47.
Parker, T.H.L.,: The Oracles of God. An Introduction to the Preaching of John Calvin. London and Redhill, 1947.
Peter, R.: unpublished Bibliography of Calvin's writings, revised by J.-Fr. Gilmont.
Realencyklopädie für protestantische Theologie und Kirche. Herausgegeben von A. Hauck. Leipzig, 1896-1909.
Registres de la compagnie des pasteurs de Genève au temps de Calvin. Edited by R. M. Kingdon and J. -F. Bergier. (Travaux d'Humanisme et Renaissance 55 and 107.) Genève, 1962, 1969.
Senebier, J.: Catalogue raisonné des manuscrits conservés dans la Bibliothèque de la Ville et République de Genève, 1779.
Stauffer, R.: Les Sermons Inédits de Calvin sur le Livre de la Genèse. *In* Revue de Théologie et de Philosophie, N.S. 98, 1, pp. 26-36. Lausanne, 1965.
—Eine Englische Sammlung von Calvinpredigten. *In* Der Prediger Johannes Calvin, pp. 47ff. (Nach Gottes Wort Reformiert, Heft 17) Neukirchen, 1966.

Index

Aesop, 146
Agricola, 131
Anabaptists, 4, 9, 19
Andrewes, 80, 137
Anselm, 80
Aquinas, 80
Augustine, 80

Barret, 69
Barrois, 75
Benoît, 75, 97, 199
Bernard, 80
Beza, 38, 73, 188, 192
Bodley, 69-70
Bonaventure, 80
Bossuet, 47
Bourgoin, 60
Brenz, 88
Bright, 66
Brooks, 45
Bucer, 131
Bullinger, 17-20, 21, 22, 27, 116, 131, 132

Cecil, R., 73
Cecil, W., 73, 191
Cherbuliez et Manget, 68, 69
Chrysostom, 80, 192
Cicero, 131
Cochlaeus, 3
Colinaeus, 87
Colladon, 57, 61, 62, 64, 119, 150, 153, 163, 164, 167

Complutensis, 87
Cop, 69
Cousin, 60, 180
Crespin, 195
Cyril of Alexandria, 88

Dallichant, 61
de Falais, 61
de la Chesnaye, 61, 160
de Normandie, 61, 154
des Gallars, 60, 61
Dodd, 35
Doumergue, 57
du Tillet, 57

Eck, 3
Edward VI, 61
Erasmus, 87, 137, 146
Étienne, H., 146

Farel, 60, 116
Fatio, 75
Field, 188, 189, 191
Forsyth, 45

Gagnebin, 69, 70, 160
Gilmont, 196
Glossa ordinaria, 88
Golding, 72, 73, 86, 190, 191, 193f.
Grindal, 191
Gueroult, 180

Hamelin Bible, 176, 177
Harmar, 73, 192
Higman, 75, 173, 174, 176, 177
Hooker, 20-21, 22, 27, 45
Horne, 73, 188, 189
Huntington, Earl of, 188
Hyperius, 132

Jerome, 88
Joinvillier, 61

Kimchi, 88

Latimer, 45, 80, 146
Leicester, Earl of, 73, 190
Littré, 46f., 141, 146
Lock, 189f.
Luther, 22, 80, 88

Maldonad, 61
Marot, 180
Mary Tudor, 65, 73
Maunoir, 69
McCord, 75
Melanchthon, 131
Michel, 177
Miles, 141, 145f.
Monod, 69
Mülhaupt, 74, 75, 148, 160
Münster, 88
Munday, 73, 189

Nagy, 75
Newman, 79, 80

Origen, 79

Peter, R., 61, 75, 182, 183, 184, 185, 186, 196
Philip of Hesse, 61
Procopius, 88
Puritans, 20, 21

Quintilian, 131

Raguenier, 65-68, 69, 70, 71, 142, 150, 153ff., 157, 158, 159, 160, 161, 162, 163, 166, 167, 176f., 178, 179, 185, 186, 190, 194
Raschi, 88
Romanists (or Papists), 10, 11, 14, 15, 19, 35, 61, 119, 122, 126f., 132
Rückert, 75

"Schoolmen", 126f.
Senebier, 68, 159
Septuagint, 172
Servetus, 142
Shakespeare, 72, 73, 146
Spifame, 61, 70
Spurgeon, 79
Stauffer, 70, 75, 190, 197
Stephanus, 87, 137
Stocker, 73, 193, 194

Targum, 88
Taylor, 146
Theremin, 69
Thorpe, 75
Tomson, 73, 74, 192
Tronchin, 69
Turks, 121, 125f.

Viret, 60, 69, 160
Vulgate, 137, 173

Warde, 73, 190
Wesley, 45
Wolf, 116

Zwingli, 17